How to Win at Interviews

How to Win at Interviews

Iain Maitland

CENTURY
BUSINESS

First published in the UK by
Hutchinson Business Books Ltd
This edition published by Century Business
An imprint of the Random Century Group Ltd
20 Vauxhall Bridge Road, London SW1V 2SA

Random Century Group Australia (Pty) Ltd
20 Alfred Street, Milsons Point
Sydney, NSW 2061, Australia

Random Century Group New Zealand Ltd
18 Poland Road, Glenfield
Auckland 10, New Zealand

Random Century Group South Africa (Pty) Ltd
PO Box 337, Bergvlei, South Africa

Reprinted 1990

This edition 1992
Reprinted 1993, 1994

Printed and bound in Great Britain by
Cox & Wyman Ltd, Reading, Berkshire

Iain Maitland has asserted his
right under the Copyright, Designs and Patents Act, 1988
to be identified as the author of this work

Random House UK Limited Reg. No. 954009

A catalogue record for this book is available
from the British Library.

ISBN 0-09-174226-9

ACKNOWLEDGMENTS

I wish to thank the following for their kind assistance:

The Metropolitan Police and, in particular, the recruiting officer at the cadet selection centre in Hendon, North London.

Wimpy International and, in particular, Barrie Hawkins and Elly Slocock.

Imperial Chemical Industries PLC and, in particular, Vivien Charters.

And finally, my special thanks to my wife, Tracey.

To Tracey and Michael

CONTENTS

Contents

CHAPTER FOUR: Types of Test

CHAPTER FIVE: After the Interview

CHAPTER SIX: Interviews at work

INTRODUCTION

Congratulations! If you are reading this, the chances are that you have applied for a job or promotion, and have shown enough promise to be invited to an interview. Well done! Whether you applied by telephone, letter, or in person, you obviously made a sufficient impression on your prospective employer for him or her to want to meet you. You are over the first hurdle . . .

. . . Now comes the difficult part. Your application impressed and stimulated interest – your interview should not only bear out that initial impression, but enhance it. It is your chance to put across those qualities (friendliness, smart appearance, ability to hold a conversation) that cannot be gaged from an application, or even a telephone call.

It is also an opportunity for *you* to investigate the organization you have applied to. Is the environment friendly and suited to your personality? Does the organization itself seem reputable and well-ordered? Is the job for which you have applied one that you would *enjoy* as well as being able to perform?

In today's job market, the idea of *you* interviewing the organization, instead of the other way round, may seem unrealistic. Indeed, in certain parts of the country, where there may be literally hundreds of applications for a single position, a mediocre employer with apparently little to offer prospective employees, may still have a choice of many able and willing applicants. But, as with job hunting, successful applicants will be those who can show that they really have made an effort to find out about the organization and the position it is offering. Applicants who reply to the question 'Why do you want this job?' by saying 'because it was the only one on offer' are unlikely to succeed. In CHAPTER ONE, we show you not only how to research the organization itself, but also the field or trade which you are hoping to enter.

By preparing thoroughly, you will have given yourself plenty to talk about at the interview, yet it is not only what you say but the way that you present yourself that will count. In CHAPTER TWO, we show you how to communicate your strengths, abilities and personality effectively, without boring the interviewer, and in a way that shows you are calm yet enthusiastic.

Of course, there will always be occasions when you are asked a question you didn't expect and haven't prepared for, or when the interviewer decides at the last moment to bring in another member of staff to sit in on the interview. You may even be unlucky enough to come up against an interviewer who is obviously so prejudiced, or just plain rude, that you feel the only thing to do is leave. We show you how to deal with these situations in CHAPTER THREE, and also give guidelines on the different types of interview you might face (panel, one to one, selection board).

On some occasions, for example when being interviewed by the Police or armed forces, you will be asked to undergo physical or mental aptitude tests. Some organizations now even insist that applicants undergo a personality test. CHAPTER FOUR shows how to find out, before the test, what might be expected of you, and gives practical advice on your approach and CHAPTER FIVE shows you how to reply to that all-important job offer.

You may think that, having followed our advice, and secured the job you wanted, you are now exempt from interviews, at least for the next few years. Not so. Once employed (or if you are already employed now), you may face appraisal, disciplinary, promotion, or even termination interviews. At the very least, there are few jobs where you will not occasionally be called upon to deal face to face with colleagues or clients, sometimes in awkward or heated situations. CHAPTER SIX shows you how to develop and adapt the skills you so successfully used in your initial interview.

PREFACE

Those of you who have already read the companion volume to this one – How to Win at Jobhunting – will be familiar with a character called David Charles. Throughout this book, I will be referring again to David Charles in order to show you, via his example, how you might prepare for, handle and follow up a successful interview.

David is a fictitious character who lives in Whittleby, Sussex. His long-term ambition is to be a sales representative. When he leaves school, Mr Kirk, the owner of Whittleby pet shop where David works as a part-time sales assistant, offers him a temporary full-time job. This will be available until David finds a permanent job that will be a step in the right direction to achieving his ambition.

David starts job hunting and, after a few weeks, he sees an advertisement in the local newspaper for a job as sales assistant in the sales office at the local Thompsons factory. Thompsons is an old-established family business manufacturing prams and pushchairs for the UK and European baby markets. It is a successful, expanding company and if David gets this job he may be able to work his way up and become a sales representative for them. He decides to apply.

The advertisement tells applicants to contact the company for an application form and then complete and return it to the personnel manager. David cycles across town to the factory, collects the application form from the personnel department and also obtains a job description and personnel specification.

1

The job description, which is often available to job hunters if they ask for it, details the main purpose and tasks involved in a job. David learns from the job description that the job's title is sales assistant and that the job holder will be responsible to the sales manageress, Mrs Bradman. The purpose of the job is to assist the sales manageress 'as required'. The main tasks involved in the job are to record, file and distribute copies of incoming sales correspondence to the appropriate persons, to record, file and despatch outgoing sales correspondence, to answer the telephone and deal with queries, to type correspondence, run general errands, and keep the office neat and tidy, and to maintain stocks of office stationery.

The personnel specification usually details the skills, qualities and knowledge required to do the job well, and is drawn up by employers to help them find the right person for the job. It may be available to job hunters if they ask for it. Alternatively, it is easy to calculate what the requirements are likely to be by carefully studying the job description.

David learns from the personnel specification that the right person must be smart, well-spoken and healthy. He or she must also have GCSE passes in English Language and Mathematics, competent typing ability and speed, some knowledge of office equipment and some previous office experience. He or she must also have common sense, a friendly manner, the ability to think quickly, and to deal with different types of people and situations. He or she must have a manual aptitude for dealing with office equipment, a verbal aptitude for dealing with people on the telephone and a numerical aptitude for adding, adjusting and totalling sales orders. Finally, he or she must also be calm, mature, reliable, dependable, methodical, conscientious and a team member.

David wants the job. He thinks he can do it well and he knows he meets the requirements. He completes the application form, making sure that he has answered all the questions concisely, neatly and correctly. He is careful to highlight his strengths in comparison with the job requirements.

He even adds an additional information sheet taking each requirement in turn and indicating how he meets it!

David then cycles back across town and delivers his completed application form. He hopes to be invited to an interview. . . .

CHAPTER ONE

PREPARING FOR THE INTERVIEW

AN INVITATION TO AN INTERVIEW

Unless you are about to be interviewed for promotion, and are already working in the organization you are applying to, your invitation to an interview will probably be either by telephone, or, more usually, by letter. In either case, the way you reply to this invitation is an important step to your success. If the invitation is by telephone, this is probably your first verbal contact with the organization you hope to work for. If it is written, your written reply is another chance to show your enthusiasm.

INVITATION BY TELEPHONE

Your invitation to an interview could be by telephone. For example, David Charles receives the following telephone call.

D.C. 'Whittleby 67082'
M.B. 'Good morning, my name's Maureen Baker from Thompsons Prams. May I speak to David Charles, please?'
D.C. 'Yes, this is David speaking. What can I do for you?'
M.B. 'It's about your application for the sales assistant vacancy. The personnel manager would like to see you. Would you be free at two o'clock on Friday?'
D.C. 'Yes, definitely. Could you just tell me the name of the interviewer and the exact location of the interview, please?'
M.B. 'Yes, it'll be Mr Tony Reynolds, the personnel manager, and the interview will be here at the main office.'
D.C. 'That's marvellous. Thank you for calling. I look forward to meeting Mr Reynolds on Friday at two o'clock at the main office.'
M.B. 'Very good, we'll see you then. Goodbye.'
D.C. 'Goodbye.'

5

David handles this brief conversation well. He is well prepared and he knows how to use the telephone. He realizes that answering the telephone is a major part of the job he has applied for. Therefore, if he is going to be invited in for an interview he expects the company to telephone to see what he sounds like and, of course, how he handles a conversation.

David answers the phone correctly with 'Whittleby 67082?'. He doesn't simply lift the receiver and wait for the other person to speak as some people do. He doesn't grunt 'allo' or 'yeah?' into the receiver either. He is correct, polite and formal. Throughout the conversation he sounds bright, friendly and confident.

He also shows he is careful and methodical. He makes sure he gets the interviewer's name. He wants to write to him to confirm the interview. This creates a favourable impression and may put David one step ahead of his rivals. David also wants to use the interviewer's name in the interview. It shows he's done his homework. It also shows respect.

David is also careful to obtain the exact location of the interview. The factory is large with many buildings and he doesn't want to make any mistakes. He concludes the conversation well. He repeats the essential points just to check he's made a note of them correctly. He is thorough.

If Mr Reynolds has asked Mrs Baker to ring each candidate to hear what they sound like then David will have created a good impression.

Invitation by letter

You may, of course, be invited in for an interview by letter. Sophie Jones, for example, receives the letter on page 19. If you receive such a letter it is important, as with a telephone call, that you make a note of all the relevant details. Make sure you know the interviewer's sex, initials and surname, and that you can *pronounce* the surname. You will want to use it in the interview.

Check the exact time, date and location of the interview. If I invited 20 candidates in for an interview when I was recruiting staff there would always be one or two who would arrive at the wrong time or even on the wrong day. One candidate once arrived in the wrong week! He knew it was a Thursday at four o'clock but wasn't sure which Thursday and 'didn't like to ask'. It's funny but far from impressive.

If in doubt, ring the company and find out. For example, Sophie didn't know the sex, initials or even the name of the interviewer. She rang the company, explained the situation and obtained the necessary information. You must do the same.

Once you've been invited to an interview you should write a short, simple letter of confirmation. It is courteous, and it may also help the interviewer to remember you. See our example on page 20.

RESEARCHING THE ORGANIZATION

All your hard work has paid off – you have progressed to an interview. You are now on the shortlist. You are very close to success. However, the really hard work now begins – you don't want to fail at this stage.

It is important that you now research the organization in great detail. There are two reasons for this:

■ To make sure that this is a step in the right direction and that you really do want to work there.
■ To show the interviewer that you have taken the trouble to find out as much as possible about the organization.

Make sure you know the answers to the following questions (some of which could be asked directly by the interviewer). The answers will then allow you to decide if this is the right organization for you and, if so, will also give you enough background information for the interview itself.

■ Who owns the organization?
■ What is its product/service?
■ How is the organization structured?
■ How many outlets/factories/offices does it have?
■ Where are they?
■ How many different departments does the organization have?

■ Who runs each department?
■ How many employees are in each department?
■ Is the organization secure and well established?
■ Is it successful and expanding?
■ What is its reputation?
■ What are its strengths?
■ What are its weaknesses?
■ What are the strengths of the product/service?
■ What are the weaknesses of the product/service?
■ How does the organization sell its product/service?
■ Who and where are its customers?
■ What is its market share?
■ Is its market share expanding?
■ What is the market itself like?
■ Is the market expanding?
■ Who are the organization's competitors?
■ What are the competitors' products/services, strengths, weaknesses, market share etc.?

You should be able to answer all of these questions if you research thoroughly. Why not visit the organization? One way of getting a look round is to deliver your letter confirming the interview in person, and ask if you can have a quick look round as you hope to be working there. Does the place seem well organized? Think about the general atmosphere. Is it friendly and happy? Would *you* enjoy working there?

Try to talk to the staff. Ask them about the organization, its products, the market and its competitors. If you have the confidence to approach them you'll often find them willing to talk. Their information can be invaluable.

Get any company literature you can. Read through company reports, brochures, catalogues, price lists and jot down all the relevant pieces of information. Memorize them for use in the interview.

Once you've obtained as much information as you can from the company and its employees why not approach their competitors? Talk to them if you can, talk to their staff and read their company literature. What do they have to say about 'your' company and its products? What do they have to say about the market?

Why not approach the trade or professional association? Visit your local library and ask to see a copy of the 'Directory of British Associations'. Find the association most relevant to your company and ring them. What do they have to say about your company or the market in general? Can they send you some literature?

Get the relevant trade or professional newspaper or magazine. The trade association you approached may, of course, send you a copy or, alternatively, tell you whom to contact. If not, go into your local library and ask for BRAD (British Rate and Data) – the relevant trade magazine should be listed in it.

Finally, try to talk to the company's customers. What do they think of the company? What information can they give you about its products?

RESEARCHING THE JOB

You should, of course, have read the advertisement and job description very carefully before applying but, before the interview, refresh your memory. Re-read the job advertisement, description, specifications, and your application. Make sure you really do want this job. Are you absolutely sure it's a step in the right direction? Are you certain that you can really do the job *well*? If you *are* certain, make sure you know what your strengths are in relation to the job. You will need to draw them into the interview at every opportunity.

You need to know the answers to the following questions (some of which could even be asked by the interviewer). The answers will allow you to decide if this is the right job and, in addition, will remind you of your strengths. The answers will also give you the necessary background information for the interview.

■ What is the job title?
■ What is its purpose?
■ What are its key tasks?

9

■ What knowledge do I need to do the job well?
■ What skills do I need to do the job well?
■ Are there any special requirements for the job?
■ What are the main terms and conditions of the job?

RESEARCHING THE INTERVIEW

It is also, of course, vitally important that you research the interview. There are several types of interview you could face (these are looked at in more detail in CHAPTER THREE).

In brief, a preliminary, or 'screening', interview may be held to reduce a long list of applicants to a short list of interviewees. A preliminary interview may be carried out by the employer or an agency. (See page 43 for further details.)

If you fulfil the basic criteria highlighted within the preliminary interview, you will probably progress to a 'one to one' or 'individual' interview with one interviewer on the other side of the desk. The interviewer will usually be the successful candidate's immediate superior, head of department, or organization's personnel manager. (See page 44 for further details, and read the David Charles interview with Tony Reynolds in CHAPTER TWO.)

Alternatively you may face a 'panel' interview – with perhaps four or five interviewers on the other side of the desk. These interviewers may consist of the company's personnel manager and your future superiors. Usually, each interviewer will be responsible for quizzing you in a particular area. (See page 51 for further details.)

In some organizations you may face a series of preliminary, individual or panel interviews as the candidates are reduced stage by stage to the final winner.

Many organizations, of course, also arrange tests to help them to decide if you are the right person for the job. (These are looked at in more detail in CHAPTER FOUR.

You may, for example, face various skills tests (see page 53) to see if you have the right aptitudes for the job. These may be manual, written or verbal.

You could also, of course, face various written or verbal

personality tests (see page 55) to see if you have the right personality for the job. The employer wants to know what you're really like and how you might react in particular situations. For organizations like the police, army, and airforce, you will probably have to face a number of physical tests (see page 57).

For some jobs, you may have to pass a medical examination. No employer wants to risk employing someone who is likely to be suddenly taken ill.

Contact the organization to find out about the type of interviews and tests you might face. They will tell you. Try, if you can, to talk to other employees who have been through the system before. They may give you some useful tips.

You should also try to find out something about the interviewer. Interviewers, of course, are all different. If you walked along your local high street and stopped ten people at random you would find that they all had different likes, dislikes, attitudes and opinions. Interviewers are the same: they are all individuals.

Some interviewers will be very good. They have been well trained by their organizations and are experienced. They are fully familiar with the types of interviews and tests that will be conducted. They have carefully studied the job description, job specification and personnel specification and know exactly what the job involves and the type of person they are looking for. They may also have an assessment form in front of them (usually based on the personnel specification) which helps them to grade you in each area. Good interviewers usually work to a plan. They know the questions they need to ask and the answers that the right candidate should give, and work loosely to this plan during the interview.

Other interviewers, of course, will be bad. Some make immediate judgments within the first few moments of meeting the interviewee. They are biased. Some are also very rude. They turn up late, don't know who you are, don't have your details and often don't seem to know what the job is either. They interrupt you, don't listen to what you say and spend the interview talking largely about themselves. Some, of course, are just inexperienced. They ask badly-phrased, garbled and confusing questions. Some are simply shy and awkward and totally unsuited to the job.

Good interviewers are easy to handle. Simply read the Do's and Don'ts of Interviewing (see below) and the David Charles interview with Tony Reynolds (page 21). Mr Reynolds is a good interviewer. Bad interviewers can be harder to handle. The Do's and Don'ts of Interviewing are still applicable though. Finally, you need to think about the types of questions you could be asked. (A list of questions is given in CHAPTER TWO.)

The range of questions is potentially endless, but most interviewers, working to a pattern, cover four main topics: home life, leisure interests, education and experience. Each question within each topic will be designed to see if you really are suitable for the job. With some questions it is easy to see why the question is being asked. For example, questions about your work experience are asked to see if you have done certain tasks before, and therefore have the knowledge and skills to do them again. Other questions are asked for less obvious reasons. For example, some candidates wonder why questions are asked about their home life (see page 24).

Read all the questions listed in CHAPTER TWO. Think why they have been asked. Think about the answers you should give. In addition, take out all the job documents again and read them through. Are there any other questions that could be asked relevant to this particular job? If, for example, the job you have applied for is a very physical one, expect several questions on your health. If your job involves handling money, expect questions on your previous cash handling experience. Think about potential questions and prepare your answers thoroughly (though not verbatim) if you want to succeed.

THE DO'S AND DON'TS OF INTERVIEWING

Whatever type of situation you face, there are a number of very simple do's and don'ts to remember. They will help you to succeed.

Do . . .

■ *Be prepared*

Always do your research. Have the facts at your fingertips. Be ready with the answers. Be ready with good questions. For example, the interviewer may ask you the question 'Tell me what you know about this organization/job?' The interviewee who is prepared can give a good answer and will probably go on to succeed. The unprepared interviewee will almost certainly fail.

■ *Be punctual*

Make sure you know exactly when and where the interview takes place. Find out how long it takes to get there. Go on a 'practice journey' if necessary. On the day of the interview add an extra thirty minutes to your journey time in case anything unexpected happens. Arrive for your interview with a few minutes to spare. Relax and gather your thoughts. Breathe deeply. Read through the job documents and company literature again. Think about the questions you might be asked and your answers. Think about your questions too. Chat to the receptionist if you can – you may pick up one or two useful snippets of information.

■ *Take care with your appearance*

You must look clean, smart and tidy. If you're a man and have a beard or moustache make sure it's neatly trimmed. Wear a dark suit, white shirt, dark tie and black socks and shoes. Such a standard, discreet 'uniform' will rarely be out of place in any circumstances. If you're a woman, you could wear a smart jacket and skirt with a matching blouse.

Avoid drinking alcohol, smoking or eating just before an interview. Drinking alcohol will dull your senses, smoking will make you smell unpleasant, and a heavy meal may make you feel uncomfortable.

■ *Relax*

You wouldn't have been invited in for an interview if you weren't capable of doing the job well. You've prepared thoroughly, you're on time and you look good. You should be relaxed. You've no need to be nervous. Make sure you look relaxed. Avoid shifting about in your chair, fiddling with pens or buttons, waving your arms about or shuffling your feet. Keep your body still throughout the interview. Hold your hands casually in your lap and tuck your legs together neatly. Lean slightly forward and look steadily at the interviewer.

Before the interview sit and look at yourself in a mirror. See yourself as the interviewer will see you. What impression will you give?

■ *Speak well*

The way you speak will indicate how you feel. Always speak in a clear, steady voice. If you hesitate or stumble you will appear nervous and ill-prepared. Never roll or slur your words. The interviewer must understand what you are saying. You must never hear the interviewer say the word 'Pardon?' Similarly, think for a second before you speak: try not to rush or gabble. Again, you will appear nervous.

Speak in your natural voice. Don't try to change it to suit the interviewer. No-one likes a 'false' voice. Avoid bad language, slang or annoying phrases or words such as 'you know' and 'actually'. Try to inject confidence, happiness and enthusiasm into your voice. Never speak in a dull monotone. Why not tape a 'dummy' interview with a friend beforehand. Play it back listening carefully to your voice and intonation. Would you want to employ a person who spoke like that?

■ *Listen to the question*

Always listen to what the interviewer is saying. Don't think about what you should have said in reply to the last question. It's too late! Don't think about what you should say in reply to the next question either. You don't know what it's going to be! Listen to the whole question NOW – not just key words in it. For example the interviewer may ask you the question 'What newspaper DO YOU READ?' If you've not been listening attentively you might miss the first half of the question and reply 'Yes, I like reading books'. Clearly, this would not impress the interviewer at all.

■ *Look at the interviewer*

Always look at the interviewer when he or she is speaking. It shows confidence and it shows you are interested in what's being said. It will also help you to succeed. For example, if the interviewer raises his eyebrows when asking the question 'Do you like *The Sun* newspaper?' it may indicate the type of answer you should give if you want to succeed. Similarly look at the interviewer when you're talking. If he or she starts shifting in his seat, looking out of the window or shuffling his papers you're probably talking too much or not answering the question. Bring your answer to a neat close promptly!

■ *Be friendly*

You may be working closely with the interviewer if you get the job so it's important that you put across the impression that you're a friendly, pleasant person. In these cases the interviewer must feel you are a person they would like to have around, all the time. Smile as often as you can without appearing false. A smile is a friendly gesture.

■ *Be polite*

Always treat the interviewer with respect and courtesy. That's simply good manners.

■ *Be calm*

Don't be distracted by interruptions. If the telephone rings or an interviewer's colleague enters the room, stay calm. Remember what you were talking about, sit back and wait for the interviewer's signal to continue talking.

Don't panic if you don't know the answer to a question. Stay cool. If you don't know the answer, admit it: 'I'm sorry but I don't know the answer to that' but do add 'but I shall find out' or 'could you tell me a little about it?'

If your mind goes blank don't worry. It happens to everyone. Simply say 'I'm very sorry but my mind's gone blank, can we come back to that point later?' Always appear calm and in control, even if you're not!

■ *Expand your answers*

Never answer a question by simply saying 'Yes' or 'No'. Show you can hold a conversation. For example, if the interviewer asks you 'Did you like your school?' don't just say 'Yes' and sit there waiting for the next question. Expand a little: 'Yes, I enjoyed it very much. It had excellent teachers and facilities'.

■ *Be positive*

Always look and sound positive. Talk in a positive manner. If you're asked the question 'Can you do this job?', the answer must never be 'I think so . . .' or 'I hope so . . .' It should be

15

'Yes I can . . .', 'definitely . . .' or 'There's no doubt about it
. . .' Never show doubt at all. You *can* do the job well.

■ *Put across your strengths*

You know what the interviewer is looking for in a candidate.
For example, she may be looking for a person with excellent
typing and shorthand speeds. You will have put this down on
your application form, CV or letter, but don't miss out on any
opportunity to stress these skills. For example, if the interviewer
asks, 'Did you like your school?' you could say 'Yes, I enjoyed
it very much. It was a good school with excellent teachers.
They helped me to achieve my typing and shorthand speeds of
60 words and 80 words per minute.' Promote your strengths at
every opportunity.

■ *Substantiate your answers*

Always support your answers with facts. For example, show
the interviewer your certificates to prove that you have the
qualifications. Prove you have done a certain task before by
explaining what you did so that it's obvious you really have. If
the interviewer asks you whether you possess specific character
traits or skills (ability to deal with pressure, ability to organize
etc), rather than simply saying yes, think of instances when you
demonstrated these abilities and talk about them.

■ *Be truthful*

Stick to the truth. A good interviewer will always uncover
a liar. (I once interviewed 62 candidates for the job of sales
representative. Some of the candidates lied. It only took a couple
of phone calls to discover that one applicant didn't have the
experience he claimed to have. It only took a simple question
'May I see your certificates, please?' to reveal that another candidate did not have the qualifications she claimed to have.) If an
interviewee claims to be able to type at a certain speed, the
interviewer need only say 'type me this letter' to see if it's true
or not.

Many of the 'Don'ts' of interviewing could of course simply
be the opposite of the 'Do's'. For example, 'Do be punctual'
and 'Do be truthful' could equally be 'Don't be late' and 'Don't

16

lie'. Nevertheless there are a number of other 'Don'ts' to consider.

Don't . . .

■ *Be a creep*
You do, of course, need to be polite and respectful. That's good manners. Don't go too far though. Some candidates commence each answer with 'Well Mr Reynolds' or 'To be honest, Mrs Fry'. They also liberally sprinkle their sentences with 'Sirs' and 'Madams'. A 'Yes Sir, no Sir, three bags full, Sir' attitude will rarely help you to succeed.

■ *Be overfamiliar*
Some candidates go to the other extreme. The interviewer may open the interview by saying 'Hello Geoffrey, my name's Jane Fry. Please take a seat.' The interviewee then moves the seat as close to the interviewer's desk as possible, and spends the entire interview leaning on it and calling the interviewer 'Jane' at every opportunity. Don't! Keep a polite distance.

■ *Drop names*
Some candidates try to impress the interviewer by constantly name dropping: 'Charles . . . that's my old boss' or 'I was talking to Jim, the managing director'. Don't. It sounds silly and immature especially from younger candidates.

■ *Criticise*
Whatever the job, you must come across as being a mature, positive person. You are an adult. Avoid criticising others. If the interviewer asks 'What do you think of your old boss?' do not reply 'He was awful. He didn't have a clue what he was doing. I did his job most of the time.' The interviewer will not be impressed. He or she won't want to be your boss! Be tactful and discreet. Show some loyalty. You could say 'I learned a great deal from him. He was the sort of man who involved me in what he was doing.' What you said is still true. You did learn from him: he showed you how not to be a boss. He also involved you in what he was doing by making you do his job!

■ *Be boring*
No-one likes a bore. No-one wants to work with one. Boring candidates talk too much and give irrelevant information. If you

speak in a dull voice you will be classified as boring even if you
are not!

■ *Interrupt*

Always let the interviewer finish his or her question. Don't
anticipate what he or she is going to say. The only time you
should interrupt is if the interviewer won't stop talking! (See
page 47.)

■ *Argue*

This seems obvious but is worth stressing. Never get into a
disagreement with the interviewer. It's unlikely you will ever
be the winner, but it's certain you will never get the job.

■ *Boast*

You should, quite rightly, promote your strengths whenever
you can but don't boast. No-one likes an arrogant candidate
who continually says 'I did this . . .' and 'I did that . . .'

21 August 1989

Miss S Jones
56 Amberley Road
Whittleby
Sussex
BN31 7AB

Dear Miss Jones

Thank you for your application of 16 August 1989. You are invited for an interview at the above address on Wednesday 30 August at 3.00 p.m.

Please telephone me on the above number should this appointment not be convenient for you.

Yours sincerely

Elizabeth Hardy

E Hardy

7 Cliff Road
Whittleby
Sussex
BN32 8NG

Whittleby 67082

30 August 1989

Mr A Reynolds
Thompsons Prams Ltd
Northbury Road Industrial Estate
Whittleby
Sussex
BN32 3LP

Dear Mr Reynolds

re: Sales Assistant Vacancy (SA7)

I am delighted to confirm that I will be attending an
interview with you this Friday at two o'clock at the main
offices.

I very much look forward to meeting you then to discuss
the above vacancy.

Yours sincerely

David Charles

David Charles

CHAPTER TWO

HANDLING AN INTERVIEW

OPENING THE INTERVIEW

One of the best ways of helping you to succeed in an interview is to, step by step, detail a real interview and then analyse it. You will therefore be able to link up the interview and the subsequent analysis with your own circumstances.

On the day of his 'one to one' interview with Mr Reynolds, David wakes early. He has taken the day off from the pet shop. He spends the morning re-reading all the literature he has on the organization and the job. He thinks about the questions he might be asked and the answers he will give. He is, therefore, well prepared.

At around midday David has a shower. He washes his hair. He puts on a new white shirt and grey tie he has bought for the interview. He also wears a black suit which he has recently had cleaned. He wears black socks and black shoes, polished the night before. He checks his appearance in the mirror. He looks neat and well-groomed.

David then decides to leave early and walk, rather than cycle, across town. He doesn't want to risk getting his clothes dirty from riding his bicycle. He puts all the job documents in his briefcase and leaves at one o'clock. He has plenty of time. He will be punctual.

David arrives at Thompsons at 1.50 pm. He feels relaxed as he is shown to a seat in reception. As he waits he catches the receptionist's eye and asks 'What's Mr Reynolds Like?' The receptionist says 'He's new. He's just joined us from McGraws, the aircraft parts manufacturer.' David smiles. He makes a mental note of this information. He then spends the last few minutes looking again at the personnel specification.

Just before two o'clock, the intercom on the receptionist's desk crackles and David hears a voice. 'Send Mr Charles along please, Miss Davies.' The receptionist points David in the direction of Mr Reynolds' office.

David knocks on the door. He waits until he hears Mr Reynolds call out 'Come in' before he enters. He looks across the room at Mr Reynolds and smiles. He shuts the door behind him *without turning his back on Mr Reynolds.*

He then walks across to the desk, still smiling and looking at Mr Reynolds. 'Hello' he says 'I'm David Charles. I'm very pleased to meet you, Mr Reynolds.'

Mr Reynolds rises from his seat. David stretches out his hand. They shake hands. David waits, for a moment, still smiling, until Mr Reynolds says 'Take a seat'. David is careful not to sit down until he is invited to do so.

David then leans slightly forward in his chair. He looks relaxed, confident and calm. He looks at Mr Reynolds who asks him if he'd like some tea or coffee. David says 'No thanks, I've just had one'. David doesn't want to try and talk and drink at the same time!

Once you've been shown to your seat, the interviewer will often start the interview by talking about the organization and/ or the job. This will usually give you a few minutes to relax. Don't just sit there though. The interview effectively started the moment you met the interviewer and these first few minutes can make or break you. Lean forward, look at the interviewer and listen to what's being said. Respond, for example, by showing you've done your homework about the organization and the job.

Mr Reynolds: 'Well David, let me firstly tell you a little about the company . . .' (David leans forward and smiles. He looks relaxed and attentive.)

'. . . Jack Thompson founded the business just after the war – 1947 to be precise. He had a young family in those days of course and thought there was a gap in the market for well made, top quality prams . . .'

(David nods in agreement. He knows this already from his research.)

David: 'Jack Thompson is Mrs Hill's father isn't he?'

Mr Reynolds: 'Yes, that's right, the old man started and ran the business up to 1976 when he retired. His daughter, Mrs Hill, then took over as managing director.'

(David nods in agreement.)

David: 'I read the company literature through before the interview so I know a little about the company and its products. Presumably Michael and James Thompson are the two sons?'

Mr Reynolds: 'That's right, you've obviously been doing your homework! I don't suppose you know who I am, do you?'

David: (laughs) 'Funnily enough I asked the receptionist about you before I came in. She told me you've just joined the company from McGraws. Aren't they the aircraft components manufacturer?'

Mr Reynolds: 'Yes. I ran the personnel department there for many years. I've been at Thompsons now for about six months. I'm going to be very busy here, we're planning to expand our British and overseas interests . . . more jobs but more work for me!'

(David laughs.)

David: 'Yes I read about the plans for expansion in *Nursery Trader*. This is obviously a go-ahead company, isn't it?'

Mr Reynolds: (nods) 'Do you know what the job entails exactly?'
David: 'I know a little. I came in before I filled out the application form to get a job description (takes the job description from his briefcase) so I've got some idea.'
Mr Reynolds: 'You know the sort of person we want then?'
David: 'Yes . . . you'll see from my application form that I've detailed the qualities you're looking for in the successful candidate and how I match up . . .'
Mr Reynolds: 'Yes . . . yes I see. Very good . . . We'll talk about that a little later on if that's okay . . . I'd like to run through some other points first though.'
David: 'Yes, of course . . .'

David handles these opening moments well. He looks at Mr Reynolds. He listens to what is being said. He looks interested. When Mr Reynolds pauses for breath, David asks a question: 'Jack Thompson is Mrs Hill's father isn't he?' David probably knows the answer already. He has done his research. However, the fact that he knows the answer is insignificant. David realizes the importance of speaking as soon as possible. He knows he must start a conversation. Candidates who sit back and wait for the first question, answer it, and then sit back and wait for the second question will fail.

David sparks the beginning of a conversation with this first question and then continues it with his second: 'Presumably Michael and James Thompson are the two sons?' He shows he is not afraid to speak. He can hold and develop a conversation which is a good quality (and, of course, a requirement of this particular job).

Throughout these opening moments David shows he has done his homework. He says 'I read the company literature', 'I asked the receptionist about you', 'I read about that in *Nursery Trader*' and 'I came . . . to get a job description'. He shows he is well prepared. He also shows he is methodical and conscientious. He obtained a job description and from this deduced the qualities required to do the job well.

If Mr Reynolds is the type of interviewer to make decisions within the first few minutes he cannot help but be impressed with David.

'FAMILY' QUESTIONS

The interviewer could then move on to ask you questions about your home life. Consider, for example, the following:

- When were you born?
- Where were you born?
- Where do you live?
- How long have you lived there?
- Do you like living there?
- Where did you live before that?
- Did you prefer living there?
- What do your parents do?
- What do they think about your application for this job?
- Do you have any brothers or sisters?
- What do they do?

The David Charles interview could develop as follows:

Mr Reynolds: (turns to application form) 'When were you born then, David?'
David: 'September 7th 1972. I'm 17 next week . . .'
Mr Reynolds: 'Congratulations . . . I see you're living up at the new Clifftops estate, do you like it there?'
David: 'Yes I do. I've got a beautiful view across the sea from my bedroom window.'
Mr Reynolds: 'Where did you live before that?'
David: 'In Shortbridge. It's a little village near Salisbury in Wiltshire. We moved here because my father was promoted. He's the manager at the local Northdale Building Society'.
Mr Reynolds: 'I see . . . what about your mum? What does she do?'
David: 'At present she's still busy with the new house. She's landscaping the garden at the moment . . .'
Mr Reynolds: 'Rather her than me! . . . what do your parents think about you applying for this job?'
David: 'I told them about my application last week. I wanted to see what they knew about the company. Background information's always useful. Anyway, I found out they bought a Thompsons pram when I was small! Mum used it for three children and my older sister's got it at the moment . . .'
Mr Reynolds: 'Sounds marvellous.'
David: (smiles) 'My dad says that if the company's as good as the pram I won't go far wrong.'
Mr Reynolds: (laughs) 'They're obviously pleased about your application then.'
David: 'Yes, definitely. They're very supportive'.

David continues to handle this interview well. He expands his answers at every opportunity. In reply to the first two questions he could simply have said 'September 7th 1972' and 'Yes' but he gives a little more to the conversation. He adds extra comments. These may appear irrelevant but they show David has the ability to chat casually and informally and to make small talk. It shows confidence. It lets the conversation flow. Again, this will be useful in the job. Don't forget that the interviewer has feelings too. He or she may be feeling nervous and awkward. If you can help the interviewer relax and enjoy the conversation they will think more favourably of you than the candidate who sits and says 'Yes . . . No . . . No . . . Yes . . .'

Expanding your answers can also help to guide the conversation into areas you want to talk about. David wants to talk about his family. When Mr Reynolds asks David 'Where did you live before that?' David steers the conversation towards his father. David is proud of his parents. His father is successful, respectable and trustworthy. David comes from a happy, contented family who are 'very supportive'. We have already discussed how interviewers judge candidates indirectly by their background and David's background is happy, solid and reliable so he tells the interviewer this.

'LEISURE' QUESTIONS

The interviewer could then ask you questions about your leisure interests. For example:

- How do you relax?
- What interests do you have?
- Do you have any hobbies?
- Do you like sport?
- Do you play any games at all?
- Do you belong to any teams?
- Do you belong to any clubs?
- Do you belong to any societies?
- What exactly do you do?
- Do you read much?
- What do you read?

- Which newspaper do you read?
- Why do you like it?
- Which page do you read first?
- What sort of books do you read?
- Who's your favourite author?
- Why do you like him/her?

Mr Reynolds: (reads application form) 'Well it all looks very promising. Tell me David, how do you relax?'

David: (smiles) 'I've not had much time this last week or so because I've been researching Thompsons. However, in my spare time lately I've been improving my typing . . .'

Mr Reynolds: 'Yes . . . yes, of course you're going to need to be able to type for this job. You probably won't have much to do but we'd certainly want to be sure you could do it if necessary.'

David: (nods) 'I see no problems at all. I can type already. I taught myself the basics and now I'm just trying to improve my speed. I want to do this job to the best of my ability so I'm going to evening classes in September.'

Mr Reynolds: 'Really? Well you can't say fairer than that . . . What else do you do David?'

David: 'Well I enjoy reading . . . not very exciting is it?'

Mr Reynolds: (smiles) 'What do you read?'

David: 'Books mainly. I enjoy thrillers and whodunnits – Ruth Rendell, PD James, that sort of thing.'

Mr Reynolds: 'Why do you like them . . . bit bloodthirsty aren't they?'

David: (laughs) 'A little . . . I don't know why I like them. To be honest I haven't thought about it . . . I suppose it's because I've always enjoyed puzzles and crosswords and these whodunnits are always a bit of a puzzle aren't they? I like to see if I can guess who the murderer is before they're revealed.'

Mr Reynolds: '. . . and do you?'

David: (laughs) 'No . . . I think if you sat down and read one from cover to cover in one sitting and actually went backwards and forwards to check what was said and who did what then maybe you could but I tend to read a bit here and there.'

Mr Reynolds: (nods) 'What about newspapers. Which one's your favourite?'

David: 'Well I read the *Whittleby Times* every day for the job advertisements and to keep up with local developments. I also read this month's *Nursery Trader* this morning to keep up with developments in this particular trade.'

Mr Reynolds: 'What about national newspapers? Which one's your favourite?'

David: 'I like *The Independent*. It's well balanced, gives both sides of the story.'

Mr Reynolds: 'What about this morning's headline? Can you remember?'

David: 'To be honest I haven't had a chance to read it yet. I spent this morning reading through the information I've gathered together on the trade, the company and the job. I also left early to make sure I got here with time to spare.'

Mr Reynolds: 'Fair enough . . . well, lets move on.'

This interview continues to progress nicely for David. He

adheres to the Do's and Don'ts of interviewing. He also shows Mr Reynolds he is the right person for the job at every opportunity. He should succeed. When Mr Reynolds asks him how he relaxes, David smiles. Do remember to do this regularly without appearing false. By smiling, David shows Mr Reynolds he is listening, relaxed, calm and friendly. All with just one gesture!

David then again reminds Mr Reynolds he has been researching the company. He shows he is well prepared. He talks about his typing which he says is 'improving'. When Mr Reynolds indicates that typing is part of the job David is very positive: 'I see no problems at all'. He substantiates this by stating that he can type already. He taught himself the basics and now wants to increase his speed. He shows he is keen to do the job well: 'I want to do this job to the best of my ability', and he proves he means this by saying 'I'm going to evening classes in September'. As Mr Reynolds says 'You can't say fairer than that'.

David again shows he speaks well and can expand his answers when he talks about reading books in his spare time. He shows, yet again, he has the ability to chat easily, which is an important part of the job.

When Mr Reynolds asks David which newspaper is his favourite David again takes the opportunity to show he is well prepared. He reads the local paper 'to keep up with local developments'. He also reads the trade magazine *Nursery Trader*. Mr Reynolds will be impressed by David's methodical, conscientious approach.

When David says he enjoys reading The Independent Mr Reynolds slips in a potentially tricky question. Does David really read the Independent or is he just saying it for effect? Does he really read one of the downmarket tabloids? David, whether he does or not, responds well. He shows he has the ability to think quickly and stay calm which are both important requirements detailed in the job specification. He carefully sidesteps the issue by stating he's spent the morning 'reading through the information I've gathered together' and, in addition, he 'also left early to make sure I got here with time to spare'. David also shows he is conscientious and reliable.

'EDUCATION' QUESTIONS

If you are applying for your first job then the interviewer will probably spend much of the interview asking you about your education, qualifications and training. For example:

- Which school/college did you attend?
- How long were you there?
- Did you like it?
- What did you most like about your school/college?
- What did you least like about your school/college?
- What did you think of your teachers?
- Which was your best subject?
- Which was your worst subject?
- Which was your favourite subject?
- Which subject did you like least?
- Why did you choose to study these subjects?
- What did you think of your exam results?
- To what would you attribute your success?
- Why did you do badly?
- What else did you do at school/college?
- Were you a prefect?
- Were you in any clubs or societies?
- Did you play for any school teams?
- What did you do during school holidays?
- What made you decide to go to university?
- Why didn't you stay on to take 'A' levels?

Mr Reynolds: 'David, I'd like to know a little more about your education. You seem to have been at a lot of different schools. Why was that?'

David: 'My father's been promoted several times and it's meant moving around the country quite a lot. We won't be moving again though. We're settled here in Whittleby.'

Mr Reynolds: 'I'm pleased to hear that, David. Do you think, out of interest, that this constant moving about affected your exam results?'

David: 'To be honest, I don't know. I certainly wouldn't want to use it as an excuse although it's true my results weren't as good as they should have been. I think this was because I concentrated on the subjects I thought were most important, such as Maths and English. As you can see from my application form I got 'A' grades in Maths and English.'

Mr Reynolds: 'Yes I've seen that. I see you actually got four GCSE's. How many did you sit?'

David: 'I also sat Geography and History. I got D grades in both. I'm planning to re-sit them both.'

Mr Reynolds: 'Why?'

David: 'Well I take pride in my work. I'm usually fairly conscientious but I didn't study as hard as I should have done for them because I concentrated on getting good English and Maths grades. I'd like to pass Geography and History if I can to prove to myself that I can do it.'

Mr Reynolds: 'What did you think of your teachers at school?'

David: 'They were very good, very helpful. My maths teacher generously gave me extra tuition at lunchtimes which I'm sure helped me to get a grade A.'

Mr Reynolds: 'What did you do in your spare time at school?'

David: 'I played chess for the school team. I'm a good team man. We won the schools league last year.'

Mr Reynolds: 'It sounds as though you're very good.'

David: 'I'm quite good. There were quite a few better than me in the team but I think I helped us to win . . . I also played tennis which was great fun.'

Mr Reynolds: 'Any good?'

David: 'To be honest, no! . . . but I enjoyed it which was the main thing. It kept me fit as well.'

Mr Reynolds: 'I'm a rugby man myself . . . do you play?'

David: 'I did when I was at my first senior school but the other schools I went to played football rather than rugby which was a pity.'

Mr Reynolds: 'You didn't think of joining a club perhaps?'

David: 'Do you know of any round here?'

Mr Reynolds: 'Yes, I run the local team as a matter of fact . . .'

David: 'Perhaps I could come along one night . . .?'

Mr Reynolds: 'Mmm, good idea . . .'

David continues to do well. Mr Reynolds, not surprisingly, asks David why he has been at several schools. It may have crossed his mind that David had been expelled. David briefly explains the situation. He avoids being boring. He doesn't talk endlessly about each school. He keeps his explanation short and snappy. He also cleverly adds the comment 'We're settled here in Whittleby'. Mr Reynolds will obviously not want to employ someone who may be moving again in six months time. David realizes this and puts his mind at ease.

Mr Reynolds then asks David if he thinks the constant moving affected his exam results. David admits that he thinks his results could have been better, which shows he is honest, but he doesn't seek to blame others, which shows he is mature. He states that he thinks the reason his results weren't as good as he hoped was that he concentrated on getting good grades in

Maths and English. He cleverly draws attention to his strengths. After all, the job specification said that the successful candidate should have 'GCSE passes (C grade or above) in English Language and Maths'. David has 'A' grades. David shows he has the ability to think quickly. He moves from a 'weakness' to a 'strength' very quickly.

Mr Reynolds probes a little further though to ask how many exams David sat. David, at this point, had carefully glossed over his Geography and History failures. However he again handles the question well. He doesn't make comments such as 'my teachers weren't very good' or 'the exam was exceptionally hard'. He admits it was his fault, because he concentrated on Maths and English Language (cleverly referring to his strengths again!), but he intends to re-sit. He shows he takes pride in his work and is conscientious. These are both impressive qualities.

When Mr Reynolds mentions David's teachers, David takes the opportunity to praise them. He again shows he is mature. He doesn't blame or criticise. (He also, yet again, refers to his Maths 'A' grade).

When Mr Reynolds asks David what he did in his spare time at school, David takes the opportunity to say 'I'm a good team man' when he mentions the school chess team. He really is on the ball. He has remembered that being a 'team member' was listed on the personnel specification and he therefore specifically mentions this.

He continues the conversation (because that is what it has now become) by showing he is modest when he talks about the chess team's success: 'I'm quite good. There were quite a few better than me.' No-one likes arrogance or conceitedness and David is careful to avoid giving that impression. He also shows again that he is a team man by saying 'I helped us to win'. He also, incidentally, shows Mr Reynolds he has 'social interests' (as detailed in the personnel specification). He plays tennis for fun.

Finally, David again shows he has the ability to think quickly. Mr Reynolds says he is 'a rugby man'. Whether he likes it or not, David decides that he will give the impression he likes rugby too. He obviously wants to impress and get on well with Mr Reynolds. As you can see, he succeeds.

'EXPERIENCE' QUESTIONS

Obviously, if you've got a job, much of the interview will
centre around your work experience. You may be asked:

- How did you get your present/last job?
- What exactly do you do?
- Tell me what you do in an average day?
- What do you like most about the job?
- What do you like least about the job?
- Which parts of the job do you find difficult?
- What's the hardest thing you've had to do?
- What have you achieved in the job?
- What have you failed to achieve in the job?
- What do you think of your boss?
- What are his/her good points?
- What are his/her bad points?
- Could you do his/her job better?
- What do you think of your colleagues?
- What do they think of you?
- What does your boss think of you?
- How much do you earn?
- Why do you want to leave?

Questions about the work you have done will often lead on to
questions about the work you hope to do in this organization,
such as:

- Why do you want to join this organization?
- What do you know about this organization?
- What do we do here?
- Tell me what you know about our product/service.
- What do you know about this job?
- What qualities do you need for this job?
- What can you offer us?
- Why should we employ you?

Mr Reynolds: 'Tell me about this part-time job of yours, David.'
David: 'What exactly do you want to know, Mr Reynolds?'
Mr Reynolds: 'How did you get it?'
David: 'Well, we moved to Whittleby last September and I decided that I
wanted a part-time job. I've always liked animals and I also wanted a job where

I'd meet different types of people so I thought of working in a pet shop. I visited every one in the area to speak to the owners and, fortunately, Mr Kirk at the Whittleby Pet Shop had a vacancy.'

Mr Reynolds: (nods) 'Good . . . what exactly do you do there?'

David: 'I'm employed as a sales assistant and I'm responsible for a number of things. Firstly I'm responsible for keeping the shop and the animals clean. Mr Kirk takes pride in having a smart, neat shop. I'm also responsible for making sure that the shelves are always fully stocked.'

Mr Reynolds: 'And if they're not?'

David: 'I make a note for Mr Kirk who will then add the items to his list for when he goes to the cash and carry.'

Mr Reynolds: 'What else do you do?'

David: 'I serve customers of course. I enjoy that very much. I help them if they have any queries. I tell them about the pets, how they should be looked after, what they eat.'

Mr Reynolds: 'Do you know a lot about animals then?'

David: 'I didn't when I started but when the shop was quiet I read as much as I could about the different animals so that I could help customers. I try to be conscientious in my work.'

Mr Reynolds: 'Good . . . good. I see from your form that you also answer the telephone. That's an important part of this job you know.'

David: 'Yes I read as much as I could about this job before I applied. I'm very familiar with the telephone. I speak clearly. I listen and, of course, I get on well with different types of people.'

Mr Reynolds: (nods) 'What do you most like about this part-time job of yours then?'

David: 'Meeting different people. There's a lot of variety in a pet shop. Some days I'll be helping a customer choose the right pet for their child. On other days I'll be dealing with a complaint.'

Mr Reynolds: 'Can you handle that?'

David: 'Yes I get on very well with all sorts of people. We don't, of course, get too many complaints because we try to satisfy every customer before they leave the shop. That's very important.'

Mr Reynolds: 'What do you like least about the job. Cleaning out the animals?'

David: (laughs) 'Well, I don't mind that really. Someone has to do it and I am the junior so I guess I'm the lucky one!'

Mr Reynolds: (laughs) 'What's your boss like?'

David: 'Mr Kirk? He's very nice. He treats me well. I have my own key and open and close the shop sometimes. He trusts me.'

Mr Reynolds: 'Well, you're obviously a responsible young man. Why do you want to leave?'

David: 'I'm very happy there, I enjoy my work. I get on well with Mr Kirk and the other part-timers but I want to progress. I'm interested in Sales. I want to join a large, expanding organization.'

Mr Reynolds' first question 'Tell me about this part-time job of yours, David?' is rather vague. Don't forget, of course, that the interviewer is human too. He or she will not always ask perfect questions. David wants to know what particular aspect Mr Reynolds is interested in so he asks him 'What exactly do you want to know?' He adds 'Mr Reynolds' to show he is polite and respectful.

David continues to give a concise explanation about how he got his part-time job. He mentions he wanted a job where he'd 'meet different types of people' which is, of course, an important part of the job he has applied for. David shows he is methodical and, indeed, hardworking: 'I visited every one in the area'. He also shows that he is confident. As you may know it takes courage to walk into a strange environment and ask for work.

When Mr Reynolds asks David what he does in his part-time job, David highlights his strengths and suitability for this job. He says he is responsible for 'keeping the shop and the animals clean'. In this job he will need to 'keep the office neat and tidy'. David also says he is responsible for making sure that 'the shelves are always fully stocked'. In this job David will need to 'maintain stocks of office stationery'. What better way of showing you can do a job than by showing you do those tasks already?

David continues by talking about serving customers which he enjoys – again, an important part of this job. He also shows he is conscientious by stating that 'when the shop was quiet I read as much as I could about the different animals'. To reinforce the point he also says 'I try to be conscientious'.

When Mr Reynolds mentions the telephone David picks up on the phrases in the job specification. He says he 'speaks clearly', 'listens' and, of course, gets on well with different types of people ('communicates').

Obviously part of this job may be to handle complaints. Every organization receives them. David confirms he can handle them. Another positive impression is given to Mr Reynolds.

David shows he is mature through his attitude to cleaning out the animals. 'Someone has to do it and I am the junior'. This also indicates he is a good team member.

David rounds up this section by praising his boss and colleagues. He shows he can fit in and get on well with people. He also shows he is ambitious: 'I want to progress . . .'

Mr Reynolds: 'Well that about covers your work experience so far but let's just look to the future a little shall we?'

David: (nods)

Mr Reynolds: 'I'd like to talk about this particular job.'

David: (nods again)

Mr Reynolds: (smiles and then laughs) 'I'm trying to think of a question. At this stage I'd normally ask something like "What do you know about this company? or what do you know about our products?" but I think you know the answers to those already don't you?'

David: (smiles) 'I hope so. As I say I obtained some literature on the company (takes brochures and price lists from his briefcase). I'm very familiar with them. I obtained the job description too so I know what the job involves. From this I worked out the qualities the successful candidate should have and I've got those qualities.'

Mr Reynolds: (nods) 'Okay David, well instead of the usual "Do you know who the owner is?" or "What do we make?" let me ask you something different. "What qualities does the successful candidate need to have?"'

David: (smiles) 'Well, the successful candidate needs many qualities. Briefly though I think it's most important that he or she gets on well with different types of people. I do. My boss at Whittleby Pet Shop will confirm that. As much of the job involves using the telephone it's also important that he or she speaks well and is able to listen. I think I speak well and I also listen to what people say. There's also a lot of writing involved in the job so the ability to write well is important. As you can see from the additional information sheet I've attached to the application form my writing is neat and tidy.'

Mr Reynolds: 'Good . . . you've summed that up nicely. I've got a personnel specification here and I've been ticking off each of the requirements wherever I think you fill them. Out of interest, let me ask you this David. Do you think you are a team member?'

David: 'Yes I do. I'm a good team man. I was part of the school chess team which won the local league. I played my part in that success. I'm also very much a member of a team at the pet shop. We all pull together in order to succeed.'

Mr Reynolds: 'Are you reliable?'

David: 'Yes I am. I've missed very few days at school and none at work. My referees, Mr Kirk and my headmaster Mr Hunt, will confirm that. I'm always on time for work, I work hard and to the best of my ability. I do what I say I'm going to do.'

Mr Reynolds: 'Would you say you are calm?'

David: 'Yes, definitely. I stay cool at all times. If we ever have a complaint at the pet shop I always remain polite, respectful and in control. You should never lose your temper. Mr Kirk will confirm I stay calm in a crisis.'

Mr Reynolds: 'Now I've got here that the successful candidate should have a numerical aptitude for adding, adjusting and totalling sales orders! Do you have a numerical aptitude?'

David: 'Yes I'm good at Maths. As you know I got an 'A' grade in my GCSE. I've the certificate here to show you' (takes it from his briefcase).

Mr Reynolds: 'Good . . . good. Well that all seems to be in order.'

At the beginning of this section Mr Reynolds is trying to think of the next question. Don't forget he's human too! David stays calm. He looks. He listens. He nods to show he is attentive. He waits for Mr Reynolds to speak.

When Mr Reynolds indicates that he thinks David already knows about the company and its products, David agrees. He again shows he is methodical and conscientious by referring to (and showing) the literature he has obtained. He again states he has 'worked out the qualities the successful candidate should have'. By expanding his answers we can again see that David is helping to guide the conversation. He wants to talk about the type of qualities required so he can talk about his strengths.

Mr Reynolds follows David's lead and asks him 'What qualities does the successful candidate need to have?' David then has a difficult decision to make. He has a lot of qualities to choose from. If he took each point in turn from the job and personnel specification he had drafted then he could talk indefinitely. He does not, however, want to appear boring. No-one likes a bore.

David therefore picks out two or three of the most important qualities required. He links them up to himself. For example, he says that 'the ability to write well is important'. He then shows the handwritten additional information sheet, supplied with his job application, which will show that this is one of his strengths.

Mr Reynolds then moves on to ask David a number of questions which directly relate to the personnel specification in front of him. He has probably already decided that David is a 'team member', is 'reliable', 'calm' and has a 'numerical aptitude', but he nevertheless wants to see what David says in reply to his questions.

David answers these questions well. He is always very positive: 'Yes I do', 'Yes I am', 'Yes, definitely' and 'Yes I'm good at Maths'. He sounds very confident and sure of himself. Each time he expands his answers and he also substantiates his statements. For example, he explains he has a numerical aptitude. He has an 'A' grade GCSE Maths. He then proves this by showing Mr Reynolds the certificate.

TRICKY QUESTIONS

Most interviewers will have a few tricky questions up their sleeves. The following ones tend to crop up regularly in most interviews at one point or another.

- How much money do you want?
- Why have you left this section blank?
- Were you sacked?
- Sell me this!
- What would you do if . . .?
- What do you think of . . .?
- Tell me all about . . .?
- Where will you be in ten years' time?

Firstly, remember to stick to the Do's and Dont's (page 12). They will serve you well in every situation.

Mr Reynolds: 'David, tell me . . . how much money do you want?'
David: 'Well at this stage in my career, money is not my main motivation. At present, it's more important that I join a good company which offers me a challenging job and good, long-term prospects.'
Mr Reynolds: 'Where do you want to be in ten years' time then?'
David: 'Well I'm quite ambitious and as Thompsons are expanding and offer excellent opportunities I would hope to be progressing with Thompsons in some way.'
Mr Reynolds: 'In what area . . . personnel? Do you want my job?'
David: (laughs) 'No . . . no, I doubt I could do your job as well as you. No, my main interest is in Sales. I like meeting people so I think that's where my interests lie.'
Mr Reynolds: 'Really? Do you see my pen? Sell it to me.'
David: (picks up Mr Reynolds' pen. He sees it is an inexpensive disposable costing a few pence). 'To be honest Mr Reynolds I wouldn't want to sell you this pen (lays it on the desk and reaches into his top pocket) but perhaps I could interest you in this (takes out an expensive fountain pen). This is your sort of pen. It's well made, classy and writes well. Let me show you . . . Now compare it with your own pen . . . There, see the difference? Why, it's like comparing a Thompsons pram with a Starling pram.'
Mr Reynolds: (laughs) 'You've obviously researched our competitors too.'
David: (nods) 'That's why I want to join Thompsons. They're the best.'
Mr Reynolds: 'Good. Now lets think about the sort of situations you might face in this job.'
David: (nods)
Mr Reynolds: 'What would you do if a customer rang up complaining that the wrong goods had been delivered or that they had arrived damaged?'

David: 'To be honest they should probably have been put through to "Despatch". Mr Nelhams is in charge there isn't he?'
Mr Reynolds: (nods)
David: 'Nevertheless if I was the one to speak to the customer it would be my responsibility to help them. I'd get the paperwork first to see what they should have received. I'd then ask them what they had received and make a note of that. I'd then explain that I would need to investigate the matter further before I could help them. I'd take their name and phone number and promise to ring them back. I'd then go to "Despatch", see what had happened, try to resolve the problem and then contact the customer with the solution.'
Mr Reynolds: 'What do you think of customers, incidentally?'
David: 'Well they're the lifeblood of the company. We can't do without them. The customer must therefore come first.'
Mr Reynolds: 'Good . . . yes, that's a valid point David.'

David handles these tricky questions well because he is prepared. The first question 'how much money do you want?' is often asked. It can be difficult to answer. If you state a figure you may price yourself out of a job. Alternatively you may undersell yourself. The advertisement may indicate a salary. It may be fixed. You could therefore say something along the lines of 'I'd be very pleased to accept the advertised salary'. Alternatively, an advertisement may indicate a price range. Again, you could indicate you'd be 'pleased to accept a salary in that particular range'.

However it is usually sensible to reply as David did. The money at this stage is unimportant. You are looking for a 'challenging job' with 'good prospects'.

The second question 'Where do you want to be in ten years' time?' is a classic question which is asked in most interviews. You obviously want to appear ambitious. No-one wants to employ a deadbeat. At the same time you don't want to appear too ambitious or arrogant. 'I'm going to do this . . .' and 'I'm going to do that . . .' is not the right approach. Indicate you want to progress with the company. They are, after all, a good, expanding organization. You want to play your part in that expansion.

The third question 'Sell me this!' is a favourite interviewer's question and some candidates freeze when they hear it. David does not. His immediate thought is to try to sell the pen to Mr Reynolds by highlighting its low price. However, he then cleverly decides to take a chance. He tries to sell Mr Reynolds his own pen which is 'classy' and 'writes well'. He compares the two pens to a Thompsons pram and a competitor's pram. In a similar situation you too could perhaps do the same.

Mr Reynolds then asks David a hypothetical 'What would you do if . . .?' question. Sometimes these questions are very relevant. The interviewer wants to know how you would react to a particular situation which might occur in the job. If you have prepared thoroughly, researched the job and know exactly what is involved then you should be able to give an answer as good as David's.

Some hypothetical questions, however, can be quite perverse. I have heard one interviewer ask the question 'What would you do if I told you there was a bomb beneath your seat?' It can be difficult to know how to reply to such a question. You could try humour: 'I'd tell you I'd seen it when I sat down, rolled it under your seat and it's going to explode in ten seconds'.

Your response, of course, depends on the particular situation. You can always try to link ridiculous hypothetical questions back to the job with 'Is that likely to happen much in this job?' which should bring the interviewer back to earth.

Similarly tricky questions can be those which begin 'What do you think of . . .?' Again, if they are relevant to the job as Mr Reynolds' question is then they are relatively easy to answer. Stick to your Do's and Dont's.

However I have heard such questions as 'What do you think of this business of selecting athletes for the Olympics then?' and 'What do you think of this new politician that's on the news all the time?' Both questions had little to do with the particular interview. Many candidates' eyes glaze over when they hear such questions. Often, they have no idea or knowledge of the subject and, even if they do, they're unsure what to say.

If you know nothing about a particular subject, try saying something like 'I'm sorry but I really don't know very much about that. Could you tell me a little bit about it?'

If you *do* know something about 'selecting athletes for the Olympics' or 'this new politician', but are unsure whether you should give your view for fear of offending the interviewer, you could say something like 'Well it's a very difficult situation isn't it? What do you think?' or 'He's certainly causing quite a stir isn't he? What do you think of him?' which would then give you a lead into a discussion.

Sometimes, of course, the interviewer may indicate his or her feelings by the way a question is phrased. Obviously, the 'right' answer would be clearly signposted if the interviewer said 'What do you think of the stupid way athletes are selected for the Olympics?' or 'What do you think of this dreadful new politician that's on the news all the time?' Do, therefore, listen. It will help you to answer a tricky question.

YOUR QUESTIONS

Towards the end of the interview the interviewer will usually ask if you have any questions. It is, of course, quite likely that you won't have any. You will have found out everything you wanted and needed to know during your research and the interview itself. Nevertheless you should try to think of two or three questions. It shows you are still interested and enthusiastic.

The questions you ask will, of course, depend on individual circumstances. It largely depends on what ground has already been covered. Think about asking questions, for example, relating to your future colleagues, training or, of course, the basic terms and conditions of the job. For example:

Mr Reynolds: 'David, I think we're coming towards the end of the interview now so I'd like to give you the opportunity to ask me some questions. Is there anything you'd like to know? Anything that isn't clear?'

David: (smiles) 'Well, we've covered all the important points but I would like to ask one or two questions if I may. Apart from Mrs Bradman, who I know will be my direct superior if I'm offered the job, can you tell me who else I'd be working with?'

Mr Reynolds: 'Yes . . . it's quite a small department at the moment. As you obviously know, Mrs Bradman is the sales manageress. Nice lady. We've two full-timers – Sally Thomas and Amanda Gayther; they've both been here for many years. We've also two part-timers of course . . . Geraldine Parker works during school hours because she's got two young children. Then there's Harry, Harry Sanderson. You'll like him. He's a nice old boy. He used to work for us as a sales rep but he's now retired. He helps us out every so often.'

David: (makes a mental note to talk to Harry about becoming a sales agent) . . . 'What about training? Can you tell me a little about how the company trains new employees?'

Mr Reynolds: 'Well there's not that much for you to learn really. You'll need to know a bit about our particular way of working though, how we file documents and that sort of thing . . . oh and you'll need to know who and where everybody is.'

David: (nods) 'I already know, from my research, about the company's organizational structure but I will, of course, need to know about your particular methods of, for example, filing and recording information. Perhaps Sally or Amanda could show me the ropes on the first day?'

Mr Reynolds: 'Yes . . . yes . . . good idea. Anything else?'

David: 'I don't think so. I know all about the job from my research. I know all about the company too. I think I'm the right person for the job and I hope you agree.'

David probably knows the answers to his questions already but, nevertheless, decides to ask them. He doesn't want the interview to simply fizzle out.

Both questions are intelligent and, yet again, David takes the opportunity to show he has done his research. He says, for example, 'Apart from Mrs Bradman, who I know will be my direct superior . . .' and 'I already know, from my research, about the company's organizational structure . . .'

David also concludes well. He sums up the situation neatly. 'I know all about the job from my research. I know all about the company too. I think I'm the right person for the job.' He then cleverly adds 'And I hope you agree', which almost sounds like a question. Will Mr Reynolds agree?

CLOSING THE INTERVIEW

Your questions will usually draw the interview to a close. At that point the interviewer could possibly offer you the job. It is, however, unlikely. He or she will probably have several other candidates to interview. It will take time to reach a final decision.

When the interview is ending you should behave in the same pleasant, friendly manner as you did when it started. If the interviewer does not indicate he or she has made a decision it is acceptable to ask something along the lines of 'When might I be told of your decision?' or 'When should I expect to hear from you?' Never ask outright if you've got the job, even if you think you have done well. That is rude and may be embarrassing. It could even *lose* you the job. Don't ask the interviewer how he or she thinks you have done either. It indicates that you lack confidence. You could do as David did by concluding 'I'm the right person for the job and I hope you agree' but don't necessarily expect an answer. See what Mr Reynolds does. He simply smiles but ignores the question.

Mr Reynolds: (smiles) 'Well, we'll be in touch within the next week. I've a few more people to interview yet but I'll get back to you as soon as I can.'

David: 'That's fine. Thank you very much for seeing me Mr Reynolds. I hope I've convinced you I'm the right person for the job and I look forward to hearing from you shortly' (smiles).

Mr Reynolds: 'You will, thanks for coming in.'

David: 'My pleasure . . .'

(They both rise from their seats and shake hands).

David ends the interview the way it started. He is friendly. He now leaves the office and returns home. As we shall see though, David does not then simply forget about the job (see CHAPTER FIVE).

CHAPTER THREE

TYPES OF INTERVIEW

Before we move on to look at what David does after the interview, lets look at the different types of interviews and tests you could face. This may be an appropriate moment now that you have an idea of the 'Do's and Don'ts' in practice.

PRELIMINARY INTERVIEWS

Preliminary, or 'screening', interviews may be carried out if there is a large number of potentially suitable applicants and the employer wishes to reduce this number to a shortlist of applicants who will progress to a detailed 'one to one' or 'panel' interview. (See pages 44 and 51.)

Sometimes employers will employ an agency to advertise the vacancy and then briefly interview potentially suitable applicants before passing the most promising ones on to the employer.

Alternatively, the employer may carry out the preliminary interview himself. You could be invited to an informal get-together at an hotel in the morning where various managers within the organization will chat informally to you over coffee and biscuits. Those applicants who appear most suitable will then be asked to attend a fuller interview in the afternoon or on another day.

Obviously, the main point of a preliminary interview is to quickly assess the suitability of a large number of applicants. By spending just a few minutes chatting to each applicant, the employer or the agency can reduce perhaps a hundred applicants to a shortlist of six in a few hours. To interview each applicant,

43

at perhaps 30 to 45 minutes per interview, could take a week. It is too time-consuming. However, the other extreme is to judge applicants purely on an application form, CV or letter. In certain circumstances this could mean the ideal candidate slips through the net. Preliminary interviews are, therefore, a useful part of the interviewing process. They fill a gap in the system.

The questions you could be asked in a preliminary interview will, of course, depend on individual circumstances. The employer or agency may simply want to check you have the basic qualifications and experience required. They may want to chat generally to you on a range of topics or, alternatively, could concentrate on a particular topic such as your previous work experience. A preliminary interview might be arranged simply to see how you look, speak and handle face-to-face conversations.

Whatever the individual circumstances, it is important that you approach the preliminary interview seriously and in the same way as a one to one interview. Adhere to the Do's and Don'ts (page 12).

Treat the interviewer with respect. Be well prepared. Think about the questions you could be asked – they could touch generally on all topics. They could, however, be quite detailed in one area. You do not know what to expect so prepare for every possibility.

When you answer questions you should, as with any other interview, expand your answers, be positive, stress your strengths and, where possible, substantiate your answers with facts.

Similarly, treat the interviewer with respect. You may think they are 'only' from an agency or 'only' junior management but they still hold your future in their hands. Take care with your appearance. Speak well. Look and listen to what they say. Be polite and respectful.

ONE TO ONE INTERVIEWS

One to one, or individual, interviews are by far the most common type of final interview you are likely to face (the other being a panel interview – see page 51). If you have a good interviewer who knows the job well, the type of person required and the questions to ask then you only need to adhere to the Do's and Don'ts of Interviewing (page 12) to do well. The interview between David Charles and Tony Reynolds in CHAPTER TWO is a good example of a 'good' one to one interview. Both interviewer and interviewee are professional in their approach and manner.

However, you may face a bad interviewer who is, for example, biased, rude or inexperienced. You may adhere to the Do's and Don'ts and be professional in your approach and manner but if the interviewer isn't then this can cause problems. At this point, therefore, it is worth considering the most common situations that can arise in a 'bad' one to one interview as a result of having a bad interviewer.

Some interviewers make instant decisions within moments of meeting a candidate. These interviewers 'judge a book by its cover'. In case you meet an interviewer like this, do make sure you look clean, smart and tidy. Buy a new tie or scarf. Catch the interviewer's eye by adjusting it in the early moments so he or she sees you've bought something new. It shows you've made an effort. It creates a good, immediate impression.

Some interviewers are biased. What should you do if you meet an interviewer whom you feel is biased against you in some way?

It depends, of course, on your circumstances. If you really want this job and feel you won't have to work with this person on a day-to-day basis, then you may wish to persevere. Simply adhere to the Do's and Don'ts of Interviewing (page 12).

Alternatively, if the situation is insufferable and you cannot face the thought of working with this person every day then the best thing may be simply to stand up and say something along the lines of 'I'm sorry but it's obvious from the range, style and tone of your questions that you are biased/sexist/racist in your views. I see no point in continuing this interview. Good afternoon to you.' Then leave. Don't become angry, or get involved in an argument. You could, however, write to the board of directors complaining about the interviewer's behaviour. You may be helping future candidates.

You may feel this is rather extreme behaviour on your part. I agree. You should, of course, only walk out in extreme circumstances. As an interviewee you do expect to face a number of probing questions (we discussed these in CHAPTER TWO). However there are interviewers whose style and type of questions are more than probing. These interviewers are simply biased and rude.

If you know you are not going to get this job why sit there for another 20 minutes and be humiliated? Even if you were offered the job (and if the interviewer is instantly biased against you it's highly unlikely), do you really want to work for a person like that? Your future would become a lottery. Stay polite, calm and respectful, retain your dignity, but leave.

If you are concerned that you may face an interviewer who is biased (and thankfully they are in the minority nowadays) then the following books may be useful: *Getting There: Jobhunting for Women* – Margaret Wallis; *Changing Your Job After 35* – Godfrey Golzen and Philip Plumbley; *Employment for Disabled People* – Mary Thompson. (All published by Kogan Page Ltd, 120 Pentonville Road, London N1.)

Some interviewers arrive late for the interview. If you're kept waiting stay calm and relaxed. Use that time for extra research. Talk to the receptionist a bit more. Try to find out that little extra piece of information that could be put to good use during the interview. David Charles, you will recall, found out a little about Tony Reynolds from the receptionist and used it to good effect in his interview (page 21).

When you finally meet the interviewer avoid making direct or indirect comments about being kept waiting. I know of one interviewee whose first words to an interviewer who had kept him waiting were 'Nice of you to turn up'. He said it with humour but, unfortunately, with this particular interviewer it wasn't appreciated. He didn't get the job.

If the interviewer does say 'Sorry to have kept you waiting', then your reply should be gracious. Say something such as 'That's no problem at all'. Add, of course, something like 'I used the extra few minutes for some last-minute research. I read your company's report through'. Never miss an opportunity to show you've done your homework.

Some interviewers may not know who you are when the interview starts. They've mislaid or lost your forms. Some may not even know what the job is exactly. It does happen. If you are well prepared and have taken in the job advertisement, job documents and your application form you can turn this to your advantage. For example:

Interviewer: 'I'm afraid I'm going to have to keep you waiting for a few minutes, old chap. The fellow who normally does all our interviewing has suddenly been taken ill. As we want to fill this job quickly the company's roped me in to sort things out. Only problem, of course, is that I don't really know what the job involves or the sort of person we're looking for. I've just sent my assistant across to the other factory to sort some details out for me though . . . he won't be too long.'

You: 'I can help you there.' (open briefcase). 'Here's a copy of the original job advertisement and the job description and specification. That'll give you all the information you need about the job. In addition this is a copy of my application form. As you'll see from the additional information sheet I have detailed the requirements of the successful applicant and shown you, under the headings of experience, knowledge, skills and personality, why I'm the right person for the job.'

Interviewer: 'Yes. Well that's excellent. Well done. Let's just have a look at what you've put then . . .'

By being well prepared you create a good, strong impression. You are off to a good start. You also draw immediate attention to your strengths which is, of course, good as well.

Some interviewers spend the entire interview talking about themselves. Many years ago I recall going for an interview in a bank. It was probably only the second or third interview I had ever attended. After showing me to my seat the manager said: 'I usually start these interviews with a bit of a talk about the bank itself. I always say it helps to put you people at your ease. The bank opened here about seven, no it wasn't, it was eight years ago. I've been here since it opened. I'm the manager. At that time of course I was over at the Bridgetown branch and I told my regional people that I thought this town here was going to expand. I lived here then you see so I knew a thing or two about the place . . .' Around fifteen minutes later he paused for breath. . . . 'Well that's about that then. Any questions, no? Well thanks for coming in, we'll let you know.'

Not surprisingly, I didn't hear from him. He was, of course, an appalling interviewer. He didn't ask me a single question.

He simply wanted to talk about himself. Nevertheless I consider that it was largely my own fault that I did not progress further. I simply sat there listening to him.

If this happens to you (and it is quite common) you must speak at the earliest opportunity. For example, at my interview with this bank manager I should have spoken almost immediately, perhaps like this:

Bank manager: 'I usually start these interviews with a bit of a talk about the bank itself. I always say it helps to put you people at your ease . . .'
Me: 'That's very good of you but, to be honest, I feel at ease with you already. Instead of you telling me about the bank let me tell you about it. Let me show you I'm conscientious enough to have done my homework. The bank opened here eight years ago . . .'

If I had offended the bank manager by speaking so quickly I would have soothed his feelings with the complimentary comment 'I feel at ease with you already'. I could then have showed one of my key strengths by talking about the bank. It would have shown I was conscientious enough to have done my homework (and 'conscientious' was a word included in the bank's job specification).

Obviously, if you face this type of interviewer there is a danger that he or she is going to dominate the interview by talking constantly at every opportunity. You therefore face the possibility that he or she will not have time to cover all the important points and, you may not be able to put across all your strengths.

You must, therefore, be on the ball all the time. If the interviewer starts to talk too much you must speak. Take every opportunity that you can to bring him or her back to the questions. Do this by referring to your strengths. For example:

Interviewer: 'I read somewhere or other that you play rugby. So do I. Marvellous game. Yes I've played rugby since the early 70's. I remember . . .'
You: 'You're a team man then, like myself?'
Interviewer: 'Mmm? Oh, yes always been a team man.'
You: 'So am I. As you'll see from my application form I played rugby and football for the school teams.'

As you can see, the interviewer is starting to ramble. The interviewee speaks as soon as he can. He draws the interviewer back to the matter in hand by indicating his strengths and inviting further questions in that area. You must do the same.

Some interviewers, of course, are simply inexperienced, poorly trained or completely unsuitable for the job. I knew one interviewer who was so shy and awkward that he was more nervous than the candidates. He spent each interview staring at the candidate's application form because he couldn't bring himself to look them in the eye.

These interviewers are not necessarily bad interviewers. They are not necessarily biased or rude. They do not turn up late, talk about themselves or ramble. They simply do not know how to approach interviewing correctly. They concentrate on the wrong areas and ask badly-phrased questions. A good interviewer asks questions which are designed to make the interviewee talk, for example:

■ What 'A' levels did you sit?
■ How much did you enjoy working at that factory?

Even the most nervous interviewee is forced to talk and say perhaps:

'I sat English, Maths and History.'
'I enjoyed it very much indeed.'

A bad interviewer phrases the questions differently:

■ Did you sit English, Maths and History?
■ Did you enjoy working at that factory?

The answers to these questions could simply be 'yes' and 'yes'. Not very revealing!

If, of course, you face an interviewer who simply asks questions which require Yes or No answers *you* must expand with:

'Yes, I obtained 'C' grades in English and Maths and a 'B' grade in History. They match your requirements in the job specification.'

'Yes, I enjoyed working there very much. My employer and colleagues were very good and helped me to do the job well. As you'll see from my letter, I did the same tasks in that job as I would be doing in this one.'

49

Sometimes these interviewers ask several questions in one. For example:

'You like reading then? Do you read books at all or newspapers? What sort of thing?'
Or
'You look like the sporting type. Do you like sport? Are you a rugby fan?'

Listen carefully to the interviewer. Then try to rearrange the questions in your mind quickly. Get them in the right order. Then reply, and as always, play to your strengths.

'Yes I like reading very much. I enjoy "whodunnits". Mind you, just lately I've been reading nothing but company literature and trade magazines to prepare for this interview!'

'Yes I like team sports. I'm a team man. I played football and basketball for the school.'

If you meet an interviewer who does not direct the conversation the way he or she should then you must effectively take control and lead the conversation over the main topics and your key strengths. For example:

Interviewer: 'Yes . . . er yes, well let's see what's er next . . . Um . . .'
You: 'Perhaps we should talk about my education?'
Interviewer: 'Oh yes . . . yes very good. I . . .'
You: 'Let me tell you about it. I went to Coombe Secondary School from 1982 to 1989. It was a very good school. Excellent teachers. They helped me to obtain 7 GCSE's and 3 'B' grade 'A' levels. As you'll see from your job specification I have all the necessary qualifications to do the job well. I also formed two school teams – Chess and Backgammon. I helped to set up a mini league between the local schools. We won both this year . . .'

As you can see, the interviewer hesitates uncertainly. He or she is inexperienced and unsure what area to discuss next. The interviewee therefore helps out. He takes the opportunity to talk about his education and, of course, his strengths. Be prepared to make a little speech about your main areas – family, hobbies, education and experience – in case you meet such an interviewer.

Finally, if you are worried about meeting a bad interviewer then, quite simply, don't! If you are applying to join a good company then their interviewers will all be trained. Bad interviewers are few and far between nowadays. Prepare for the one to one interview the way that David Charles did. Adhere to the Do's and Don'ts and you should do well.

PANEL INTERVIEWS

Some organizations prefer to conduct panel interviews where perhaps three or more interviewers face you on the other side of the desk. The panel could consist of your immediate superior, the head of the appropriate department and the personnel officer, but this will, of course, depend on individual circumstances. If, for example, you have applied for a job which involves specialist work then an expert in that particular field could be on the panel.

Usually each interviewer will be responsible for quizzing you in a particular area. For example, your immediate superior could start by asking you about your family and hobbies, the head of department could ask you about your education, and the personnel officer could ask you about your work experience.

Panel interviews are generally fairer to a candidate. With a 'one to one' interview you could, as we have seen, face a bad interviewer. As a result of this you may be the best person for the job but may not succeed because of his or her bias or inexperience. However with a panel of, perhaps, three to six interviewers, it is highly unlikely that they will all be bad. As the final decision will usually be reached after a discussion involving all the interviewers it is likely that if you are the best person for the job then you will succeed. Handle a panel interview in the same basic way you would handle a 'one to one' interview. Follow, as always, the basic Do's and Don'ts of Interviewing (page 12).

There are, however, a number of additional points to consider. Firstly, try to find out the names of each interviewer beforehand. Talk to the organization's employees when you are doing your research (see pages 7–12) or ask the receptionist immediately before the interview.

When you enter the room look at each of the interviewers in turn, smile, nod and say, for example, 'Hallo Mrs Reid . . . Mr

Brown . . . Mrs Seabrook'. Addressing each interviewer by the correct name will impress them.

Make sure that you look at each interviewer throughout the interview. Treat them all with equal respect. If you ignore one because he or she doesn't ask many questions you may find that he is the one whose opinion carries the most influence.

To ensure that you give each the respect and attention you should, look at and listen to the individual interviewer who is asking you a question. As you answer look at each interviewer in turn. Smile regularly at each too.

At the end of the interview you should smile, thank and shake hands with each again. Refer to them by their names. It looks and sounds professional.

If you have to face a panel interview, read through CHAPTER TWO again. Imagine that the questions are being asked by, say, three interviewers, and think how you should respond.

CHAPTER FOUR

TYPES OF TEST

School, college and university leavers usually obtain jobs on the basis of one, or perhaps two, individual or panel interviews, followed by a medical. The potentially complex area of tests will probably play no part in your interviewing process. Nevertheless it is a possibility that they will and, as such, they do need to be considered briefly.

For the sake of simplicity I intend to look at tests under the very loose and interchangeable headings of skills, personality and physical tests. Because of the enormous range of different tests applied by different organizations it is impossible to look at any of them in detail. Therefore I have looked briefly at the different, general headings and, where appropriate, have indicated where you can obtain further, detailed information. For example, I have indicated in the Recommended reading list (page 81) a book on psychological testing.

If you are to face a test, first contact the organization and find out the type of test. Talk to employees who may offer advice. Then, if appropriate, find out as much as you can about the particular tests by researching. Read the books I recommend (page 81).

SKILLS TESTS

Obviously, a straightforward 'one to one' or panel interview can, if handled well, reveal a great deal about a candidate.

For example, David applied for the sales assistant job at Thompsons Prams and the personnel specification stated that, to do the job well, Mr Reynolds noted that the successful applicant must have 'the ability to think quickly', a 'manual aptitude for using office equipment', a 'verbal aptitude for using the telephone' and a 'numerical aptitude for adding, adjusting and totalling sales orders'.

In the interview Mr Reynolds could obviously judge, for example, David's 'ability to think quickly' by his responses to questions. Similarly Mr Reynolds could judge David's 'verbal aptitude' by listening to him. Mr Reynolds could see if David had the necessary 'manual' and 'numerical' aptitudes by seeing if he had done similar tasks before which would indicate that he had those aptitudes. In addition, David's GCSE 'A' grade in Maths further indicated that he had a 'numerical' aptitude.

Sometimes, however, employers want to know exactly how good a candidate is in comparison to, perhaps, the 'average person' or fellow candidates. The employer may be able to say to him or herself 'Yes, this candidate has the ability to think quickly' . . . but how quickly? Does he or she think quickly enough? Does candidate A think quicker than candidate B, C or D?'

The employer may be able to say 'Yes, this candidate has the necessary aptitudes for the job' but may want to compare the candidate with others. After all, six candidates may all have certain aptitudes but which of the six is most suited to the job? To answer this the employer may arrange various skills tests to help him or her to decide.

An IQ test is a popular way of testing your intelligence and ability to think quickly. You will have to answer a set number of questions in a set time. Your score and IQ are then assessed and you will be compared to the 'average person'. The employer will then decide whether you are intelligent enough to do the job.

You may, of course, have come across IQ tests before at some point and will be familiar with the type of questions involved. You may, for example, be given two words such as NIGHT and HOUSE and be asked to find a word which fits between the two. Similarly you could be given a sequence of numbers such as 25, 36, 49 and 64 and be asked to list the next two. If you expect to face an IQ test buy a book on IQ tests and do as many tests as you can. Practice makes perfect.

You could face a test of your numerical aptitude if this aptitude is necessary for your job. In David's case, for example, he needs to be able to add, adjust and total sales orders. He may therefore be given a simple mathematics test to see if he can correctly answer a number of questions in a certain time.

This could be done verbally with Mr Reynolds asking David to add and subtract numbers he calls out. Alternatively, it could be in writing and along the lines of an IQ test, as already described.

You could face a handwriting test. If Mr Reynolds had not seen David's handwriting on the application form he may have asked David to write a few lines. If part of your job will involve writing then practise writing neatly and check spelling, punctuation and grammar.

You could, of course, face practical tests. To do the job, David will have to operate office machinery and be able to type competently. Mr Reynolds could have tested David by asking him to operate the office machinery to see if he could do it. Similarly he could have asked David to type a letter. Mr Reynolds could then have timed him and subsequently checked the letter for accuracy.

In similar circumstances, you should familiarize yourself with office machinery and how it works. Have you parents, friends or colleagues who can help? If you expect to have to type then practise beforehand. Brush up your skills if they are a little rusty, and make sure your typing is sufficiently fast and accurate.

PERSONALITY TESTS

In addition to testing your skills and aptitudes, the employer may also want to test your personality. Mr Reynolds, for example, may have been able to judge whether David is 'calm', 'methodical' and 'a team member' by asking him questions and listening to his answers but may want David to do further tests to confirm his opinion.

There are a number of tests which can help the employer to assess your personality. Graphology, the analysis of handwriting to reveal your personality, is becoming increasingly popular. You may be asked to supply a sample of your normal handwriting for analysis. If so, visit your local library or bookshop and read a book on handwriting. Compare the examples in the text with your own handwriting. What does it say about you? How can you improve your handwriting to indicate a better personality!

You may be asked to 'Describe Yourself' or 'Describe yourself as others see you'. If you have prepared you will know what type of person the employer is looking for exactly. You will have obtained a personnel specification (David, for example, knows the successful candidate must be calm, mature, reliable, dependable, methodical, conscientious and a team member). Your written answer should pick up on these points, expand on them and, where possible, be substantiated by attaching an additional information sheet. In his additional information sheet, David has already described himself along the lines suggested. You must do the same.

Obviously one of the best ways of seeing whether you have the right personality is to put you into a situation which you could face in the job and see how you handle it. You may recall that Mr Reynolds asked David how he would handle certain situations such as a phone call from a customer (page 36). Mr Reynolds could, of course, have tested David further by actually putting him on the telephone to see what he did. Alternatively, Mr Reynolds could have staged a series of mock phone calls to test David in a 'real life' situation.

To prepare for this type of test you obviously need to study the job description and decide what 'real life situations' you might have to deal with. Then study the personnel specification. You are that person! How would that particular type of person react in each of those real life situations? If you are right for this job that is the way you would react.

Another popular way of testing your personality, and skills, is to put all the candidates together. The group is then expected to discuss a particular subject or solve a problem. The employers will then watch, listen and assess each individual. What is your personality like? Are you a leader? A team member? In addition, do you show organizational skills, communication skills, initiative and reasoning skills?

The subject for discussion will often be something currently in the news. If the organization has told you to prepare for this type of test then do make sure you have read a range of trade, local and national newspapers over the last few days. Are there any obvious subjects that might be covered? Anything particularly topical or controversial? Make sure you have all the background information and know the arguments for both sides. Examples of Group Discussion topics are given on page 58, courtesy of the recruiting officer of the Metropolitan Police. The problem that needs solving will, of course, depend on the organization. It could be one of the hypothetical type of questions asked during the interview (see page 36).

Alternatively, the problem could be to cross an imaginary ravine with one of the group strapped onto a stretcher with, supposedly, a broken leg. This type of problem solving test is very popular in the armed forces.

In some group tests each member is given a topic and, after being given time to think about it, is asked to stand up and give a five minute talk. A list of possible topics is given on page 58, courtesy of the recruiting officer of the Metropolitan Police. If you expect to face group tests then borrow or buy the books listed in the recommended reading list and study them.

PHYSICAL TESTS

You may, of course, have to face a range of physical tests if you want to join a particular organization. If, for example, you want to join the police, army, navy or air force you will be expected to be able to swim 100 metres, run 100 metres and 1,500 metres, in addition to doing bar heaves and a standing long jump. You will of course, be timed or measured for each of these and compared to the 'average person'.

As with other tests, the best way of preparing is to contact the organization. Find out what physical tests you may have to face and find out what is considered to be a satisfactory performance. If you cannot find this information out from the organization or its employees, look through one of the many health and fitness books in your library. What is the average time it takes a fit young person to run, say, 100 metres? What is your speed? If necessary keep practising until you can achieve good results. If physical tests are part of the selection process then physical aptitude is an important part of the job. If you want the job you must prepare thoroughly.

For most jobs you will face a medical examination (see page 64). This will usually be a standard check up and should not, if you are healthy, create any problems. Talk to your doctor beforehand if you have any doubts.

(In addition to supplying examples of group discussion exercises, the recruiting officer of the Metropolitan Police has also kindly supplied examples of the types of question prospective police cadets face. These questions could be used as the basis of a group discussion or, indeed, for an individual talk.)

- Do schools do enough to prepare students for 'the outside world'?
- Should drunk drivers be banned for life?
- Should the Police be controlled by elected politicians?
- Should television sex and violence be censored?
- Would conscription cure teenage crime?
- 'You can tell what a person is like by his/her appearance' – discuss.
- Is too much importance placed on qualifications?
- Riots – are baton rounds and water cannon the answer?
- Should charities be necessary in a civilized society?
- Is the monarchy relevant in today's world?
- Unemployment – can anything be done?
- Sunday trading – would it disrupt the traditional day of worship and rest?
- Euthanasia – the case for and against.
- Proportional representation – the case for and against.
- The smoking of cannabis should be legalised – the case for and against.
- Will the use of supporter membership cards curb football hooliganism?

- Should there be a common European state?
- Do politics interfere with sport?
- Should smoking be banned in public places?
- Should animals be used for medical research?
- Bring back hanging – the case for and against.

POLICE STANDARDISED ENTRANCE TESTS

The police standardised entrance test is sat by all applicants to the police service not exempted because of their academic qualifications. Previous examination papers cannot be provided, but this sample of the types of questions asked may prove helpful to prospective applicants. The test comprises five categories, as outlined below.

A candidate may re-sit the examination, but only after a period of six months has elapsed.

INDIVIDUAL TESTS MAKING UP THE TEST BATTERY

Test 1 – Mixed Sentences

A verbal reasoning test, lasting 20 minutes. This involves interchanging two words in a sentence, to make the sentence read sensibly. (25 sentences)
Examples
1. General people who have to go into hospital are admitted to most wards.

2. It has not been said that in this country we do often like theory; we prefer to think of John Bull as very practical.

Test 2 – Verbal

An educational test, lasting 15 minutes. Given the first and last letters of a word, and a clue to what it means, the candidate has to complete the word. (75 words)
Examples
1. Cultivation of the land   A . . . . . . RE   AGRICULTURE
2. To congeal; become solid   C . . . . . . TE   COAGULATE

Test 3 – Spelling

A straightforward educational test, lasting 10 minutes. Candidates are given 4 spellings of a word and have to indicate which is correct. (40 words)

Examples

1. A Dillemma B Dilemma   C Dillema   D Dilema   Answer: B
2. A Acsident B Acsedent   C Acedent D Acident   Answer: NONE

Test 4 – Arithmetic

A test of basic arithmetic, lasting 25 minutes. (20 questions)

Examples

1. How much would 12 kilograms of tomatoes cost if one pound costs 27½p?   (1 kilogram = 2.20 pounds) .... £

2. An aeroplane flew 8 hours before reaching its destination. It changed direction twice and the distance covered on the three legs of the journey were in the ratio 1:2:3½. If the average ground speed for the journey was 520 mph, what was the distance covered on the first stage? .... miles

Test 5 – Checking

A test of accuracy, while working at speed, lasting 10 minutes. The candidate has to check whether the entries of names and addresses in two columns do or do not correspond exactly. (100 entries)

Examples

	A	B	Answer
1.	Mrs L P Cockerill 17 Woodford Road London NW1	Mrs L P Cockerill 17 Woodford Road London NW1	
2.	Mr H A Davenport 18 Abbey Road Oxford	Mr H A Davenport 8 Abbey Road Oxford	X

Courtesy of the Recruiting Officer of the Metropolitan Police.

CHAPTER FIVE

AFTER THE INTERVIEW

FOLLOWING THROUGH

After an interview it is important that you immediately review your performance while it is still fresh in your mind. How well did you do? Answer the following questions.

- Did you arrive on time?
- Did you look clean and smart?
- Did you handle the opening moments well?
- Did you feel relaxed?
- Did you look relaxed?
- Did you stay cool and calm?
- Did you stay polite and respectful?
- Did you answer all the questions well?
- Did you expand your answers?
- Did you substantiate your answers?
- Did you refer to each of your strengths?
- Did you emphasize your key strengths?
- Did you ask good questions?
- Did you handle the closing moments well?
- Did you impress the interviewer?

If you can answer 'yes' to each of the above then clearly you have done well. You have a good chance of succeeding. If you have said 'no' to any of these questions, you need to ask yourself why. How can you improve your performance for the future? Think carefully.

If you think you are in with a chance of being offered the job then you should write a follow-up letter to the interviewer.

This should thank him or her for seeing you and re-confirm your interest in the job. Mention one or two of your key strengths again and enclose any items you promised to forward such as photocopies of certificates or samples of work.

As with the letter of confirmation (see page 20) this follow-up letter could help you to stand out from the crowd. It may give you that extra edge. Type it, or, if neat handwriting is part of the job, write the letter and post or deliver it to the organization on the same day as the interview. Be first. Show you're still enthusiastic and keen. If you really do want the job, prove it!

David reviews his performance after his interview with Mr Reynolds. He thinks he can answer 'yes' to each question but isn't absolutely sure whether he referred to each of his strengths for this job. He looks at the job advertisement, job description and specifications when he gets home and checks. He's fairly sure he did refer to each of his strengths but decides that when he writes his follow-up letter he'll refer to them all again generally anyway. David then sits down and writes the letter on page 63. Afterwards he cycles back to Thompsons factory and hands the letter to the receptionist.

Once you've reviewed your performance and written your follow-up letter you should then put all thoughts of the job to one side again (the way that you did after you had submitted your original application). Continue job hunting and, hopefully, continue attending interviews.

It will, of course, take time for the interviewer to reach a decision. There may be other candidates to see or other people to consult. Mr Reynolds, for example, will want to discuss the candidates with Mrs Bradman, the sales manageress. Never chase the interviewer for a decision. Subsequent letters or telephone calls will harass and annoy, and may damage your chances of success.

RECEIVING A JOB OFFER

At some stage you will hear from the organization. You may perhaps be rejected. If you are, then read those questions again.

7 Cliff Road
Whittleby
Sussex
BN32 8NG

Whittleby 67082

1 September 1989

Mr T Reynolds
Thompsons Prams Ltd
Northbury Road Industrial Estate
Whittleby
Sussex
BN32 3LP

Dear Mr Reynolds

re: Sales Assistant Vacancy (SA7)

I thought I would just write to thank you for seeing me
this afternoon with regard to the above vacancy.

I confirm I would very much like to be offered the job. As
detailed in my additional information sheet I have all the
experience, knowledge, skills and personality required to
do the job well. I would be an asset to your company.

Once again, thank you for seeing me and I look forward
to hearing from you shortly.

Yours sincerely

David Charles

David Charles

Why do you think you failed? If you got on well with the interviewer telephone and ask why you were turned down. They may, off the record, tell you, which would be of immense benefit to you in the future.

Of course, you may have done everything right. You may have answered 'yes' to each question when you reviewed your performance but still have been rejected. There may simply be only one vacancy and, therefore, only one winner. Perhaps you were excellent, but so was someone else. If you think this is the case ask if there are any other vacancies you might be considered for. If not, ask for your name, address and details to be kept on file. Then write regularly to remind the interviewer that you're still interested in working for the organization. Perseverance sometimes pays off.

Hopefully, of course, you will receive an offer of employment. This offer will usually be conditional, subject to satisfactory references and passing a medical. Mr Reynolds sends David a written offer of employment (see page 65).

Once you have received a conditional offer of employment you must decide if you want to accept. You may, for example, be in the fortunate position of being offered several jobs. If you decide to reject the offer you must contact the organization immediately, preferably by telephone, thanking them for the offer but explaining that you have been offered another job which you wish to accept. Be careful not to offend them. You may, one day, cross paths again. Be polite and respectful. The job you are rejecting was excellent but the one you are accepting is, perhaps 'closer to home' or 'more suited to my capabilities'.

If you wish to accept the offer, you should again contact the organization immediately. Telephone and confirm that they may approach your referees. Arrange a medical. If you have any questions about the job take the opportunity to ask them now. For example:

- What exactly is my job?
- Where exactly will I work?
- Who will be my immediate superior?
- How much will I be paid?
- How often will I be paid?

THOMPSONS PRAMS LTD

Northbury Road Industrial Estate
Whittleby, Sussex
BN32 3LP   Tel Whittleby 67111/2/3/4

5 September 1989

Mr D Charles
7 Cliff Road
Whittleby
Sussex
BN32 8NG

Dear David

It was a pleasure to meet you on Friday and I am now
pleased to offer you employment as a sales assistant in
our main sales office at a commencing salary of £125 for
a 35 hour week. Your hours will be from 9am to 5pm
from Monday to Friday with a one-hour lunch break
taken when convenient to Mrs Bradman, the sales
manageress. This offer is conditional and is subject to
satisfactory references from your two referees and a satisfactory medical examination.

Please will you confirm that we may approach Mr Kirk
and Mr Hunt for references and will you also contact Dr
Wakefield, our medical officer, to arrange a convenient
time for your medical examination.

Yours sincerely

Tony Reynolds.

T Reynolds

■ How will I be paid?
■ What will be my hours of work?
■ Will there be overtime?
■ How many holidays will I have per annum?
■ Will I have to work bank holidays?
■ Will I be paid for holidays?
■ How do I choose my holidays?
■ What happens if I am ill?
■ Whom do I contact?
■ Will I be paid if I am ill?
■ Is there a pension scheme?
■ What are the company's rules, regulations and procedures?
■ Who do I speak to if I have a problem?

Then, of course, contact your referees and tell them that the organization will shortly be approaching them. That is courteous. Assuming that references and the medical examination both prove satisfactory you will then receive a formal written offer of employment.

David receives Mr Reynolds letter. He telephones Mr Reynolds to confirm his referees may be approached. He then telephones Dr Wakefield to arrange for a medical examination. David does not need to ask any additional questions about the job. He knows all the answers already from his research.

David tells Mr Kirk that Thompsons Prams have offered him a job. Mr Kirk is very pleased and promises to give him a good reference. David then telephones Mr Hunt and explains about the job. Mr Hunt also promises to give him a good reference. David thanks him.

David's references are exemplary and his medical proves to be satisfactory. He therefore subsequently receives a formal, written offer from Mr Reynolds (see page 68).

Once you have received this formal offer you can, assuming you wish to accept, stop job hunting. If you have a job you can also hand in your notice. If you resign from a job do it graciously. Don't use it as an opportunity to settle old scores or to tell your bosses what you really think of them. Act as an adult and with dignity. If that is not sufficient reason, bear in mind that if you create bad feeling when you leave it could rebound on you. Think of what might happen if, for example, your old employer knows your new employer socially? The effect could be disastrous. If you resign from a job go to your employer and tell him or her that you are leaving, and before you resign take a look at termination interviews on page 77.

David leaves Whittleby pet shop on good terms. He is friendly with Mr Kirk and wishes to remain that way. If things don't work out for him at Thompsons Prams he may want to return.

Finally, of course, you must also contact your new employers to accept the offer and to confirm you can start on the agreed date. You will normally be asked to accept and confirm this in a letter (see David's letter on page 70).

STARTING WORK

You are now ready to start work on the agreed date. You have succeeded! Now, you face a bright new future in a new organization. However, you will probably still have to face further interviews once you have started work. There may be interviews to discuss grievances or discipline. There may be regular appraisal interviews to evaluate your work. You may have to face a rigorous series of interviews if you want to be promoted. You may even be interviewed if you resign or are dismissed. Do not, therefore, forget the interviewing skills and knowledge you have acquired. As you will see from CHAPTER SIX, you will always need them.

THOMPSONS PRAMS LTD

Northbury Road Industrial Estate
Whittleby, Sussex
BN32 3LP   Tel Whittleby 67111/2/3/4

8 September 1989

Mr D Charles
7 Cliff Road
Whittleby
Sussex
BN32 8NG

Dear David

I write to confirm that my conditional offer of employment of 5 September 1989 is now definite. Your references and medical were satisfactory. If you accept this
offer the following terms and conditions will apply:

1. Your employment will commence on 18.9.89.

2. You will be employed as a sales assistant at our main
   sales office at the above address.

3. You will be paid £125 per week. This will be paid in
   arrears on the 15th day of each month following the
   month you start work. Your salary will be paid
   directly into your bank account.

4. Your normal working hours will be from 9.00am to
   5.00pm from Monday to Friday inclusive. You will
   take a one hour lunch break at your superior's convenience. Overtime will not be available.

5. You will be entitled to 20 days paid holiday plus paid public holidays each calendar year. Holidays will be taken at the company's convenience.

6. You will be paid statutory sick pay according to current statutory rules and regulations (see enclosed company handbook).

7. There is no pension scheme.

8. You will be required to give us one week's notice if you wish to terminate your employment. We will be required to give you notice according to current statutory rules and regulations (see enclosed company handbook).

9. Disciplinary rules and procedures are detailed in the company handbook.

10. Grievance rules and procedures are detailed in the company handbook.

I look forward to meeting you again on 18 September.

With very best wishes for the future,

Tony Reynolds.

T Reynolds

Enc.

7 Cliff Road
Whittleby
Sussex
BN32 8NG

Whittleby 67082

8 September 1989

Mr T Reynolds
Thompsons Prams Ltd
Northbury Road Industrial Estate
Whittleby
Sussex
BN32 3LP

Dear Mr Reynolds

Many thanks for your offer of employment of the above
date. I am pleased to accept the terms and conditions
outlined in the letter and to confirm that I can start work
at 9am on Monday 18 September.

I look forward to meeting you again in due course.

Yours sincerely

David Charles

David Charles

CHAPTER SIX

INTERVIEWS AT WORK

The Do's and Don'ts of Interviewing (CHAPTER ONE) still apply to interviews at work. Before reading this chapter, remind yourself of the Do's and Don'ts again.

DISCIPLINARY INTERVIEWS

Disciplinary procedure will, of course, vary between organizations. You should be aware of procedure in your own organization. Minor disciplinary matters will usually be dealt with on an informal oral basis. For example:

Mrs Bradman: 'Ah, David, glad I've caught you. I wanted a word. Come into my office.'

David: (smiles and follows Mrs Bradman into her office).

Mrs Bradman: 'Take a seat.'

David: (smiles and sits down) 'Thank you.'

Mrs Bradman: 'Now then, David. You seem to have been late for work three times this week already. Why is that?'

David: 'I'm sorry. I overslept on Monday and Tuesday and yesterday the bus was late. However, I've just bought a new mini alarm clock (shows it to Mrs Bradman) and I also intend to catch the earlier bus from now on.'

Mrs Bradman: 'I see. Well I accept your explanation, David. Thank you for telling me. It won't happen again then?'

David: 'No, definitely not.'

Mrs Bradman: 'Good, that will be all then, thank you David.'

David: (smiles) 'Thank you Mrs Bradman.'

Assuming David is not late again, nothing more should be said. He handles this conversation well. He is polite and friendly. He does not sit down until Mrs Bradman says 'Take a seat'. David also smiles regularly. It is a friendly gesture.

When Mrs Bradman asks him why he has been late three times already that week David does not blame others. He does not disagree, contradict or argue with Mrs Bradman. He knows he is in the wrong. He has made a mistake. He admits he is at fault.

David immediately starts by saying 'I'm sorry'. This takes the heat out of the situation. David explains why he has been late, succinctly and concisely. He then explains how he will rectify his mistake – 'I've just bought a new mini alarm clock', 'I intend to catch the earlier bus from now on'. He also substantiates his answer by showing Mrs Bradman the mini alarm clock he has just bought. When Mrs Bradman asks 'It won't happen again then?', David is positive – 'No, definitely not'. He also adopts a positive attitude when he leaves. He smiles and says 'Thank you, Mrs Bradman'.

Of course, some disciplinary interviews may be of a more serious nature. As such you should immediately seek advice on your individual circumstances from your local Citizens Advice Bureau, your solicitor, ACAS or the Department of Employment.

APPRAISAL INTERVIEWS

The purpose of an appraisal interview is to evaluate an employee's work performance over a period of time and, by identifying the employee's strengths and weaknesses, to improve his or her performance for the future.

Appraisal, or 'progress', interviews are a regular feature in most organizations. They may be held annually or, for new employees, on a quarterly basis. You should know what happens in your own organization. An appraisal interview will usually take place with your immediate superior, head of department or the personnel manager. Before the interview your immediate superior will normally complete an appraisal form on which your performance will be graded in a number of areas.

For example, Mrs Bradman may have to complete the appraisal form on page 73 for David. (Your immediate superior will probably complete a similar one on you).

APPRAISAL FORM

NAME:

JOB TITLE:

DEPARTMENT:

COMMENCED WORK ON:

PLEASE TICK WHERE APPROPRIATE

	UNSATIS-FACTORY	SATIS-FACTORY	VERY GOOD	EXCELLENT
ATTENDANCE				
COMMENTS				
RELIABILITY				
COMMENTS				
WORK				
COMMENTS				
PERSONALITY				
COMMENTS				
PROGRESS				
COMMENTS				

SIGNED   DATE

Mrs Bradman asks herself these questions about David before completing the form. (Your superior will probably consider similar questions.)

- Has David's attendance been unsatisfactory, satisfactory, very good or excellent?
- Has he been off sick at any time?
- Was this certified or uncertified?
- Have there been any unexplained absences?
- Is David reliable?
- Does he turn up for work on time?
- Does he do what he promises to do?
- Is David's work unsatisfactory, satisfactory, very good or excellent?
- Can he record, file and distribute copies of all incoming sales correspondence correctly?
- Can he record, file and despatch outgoing sales correspondence correctly?
- Can he answer the telephone and deal with telephone queries?
- Does he liaise well with other departments?
- Does he type well?
- Does he keep the office neat and tidy?
- Does he maintain stocks of office stationery?
- Does he have a thorough knowledge of all aspects of the job?
- Does he have all the skills required to do the job well?
- Is his personality right for the job?
- Is he smart?
- Is he well-spoken?
- Is his health good?
- Does he think quickly?
- Is he calm?
- Is he mature?
- Is he methodical?
- Is he conscientious?
- Is he a team member?
- Is he progressing?
- Is he developing his strengths?

■ **Is he eliminating his weaknesses?**

After completing David's appraisal form, Mrs Bradman passes it on to Mr Reynolds who conducts an appraisal interview.

Mr Reynolds: 'Come in David, take a seat . . . how are you getting on?'

David: (smiles) 'Very well, thank you Mr Reynolds. I'm very happy here.'

Mr Reynolds: 'Thats good . . . good. Well, look, I've asked you to pop in for a chat so we can just talk about your performance to date. We regularly appraise each of our employees every year just to see how they're progressing, whether they're happy, have any problems and so on. With new employees we have one of these little meetings after six months.'

David: (smiles) 'Now it's my turn then!'

Mr Reynolds: 'That's right . . . Mrs Bradman's filled out an appraisal form on you. I'll show it to you (passes the form to David). As you can see we keep these forms very broad and generalised in this company . . . anyway, Mrs Bradman's marked you as . . . let me see . . . excellent under "attendance", very good under "reliability", satisfactory under "work", very good under "personality" and very good under "progress".'

David: 'Yes, I see. However I also see, under comments for "work", that my recording and filing of documents is suspect. May I explain?'

Mr Reynolds: (smiles) 'Of course, I was going to mention that myself.'

David: 'Well, as you know, Mr Reynolds, the company has just been computerised. Unfortunately, I was off sick on the day the training seminar was held for the staff. Mrs Bradman has subsequently shown me how to work the computer and, under supervision, I work well. However, I have made a number of mistakes when working on my own. I have just bought a handbook on the subject though (takes it from his briefcase) and I have also booked a one-day computer course at the local college next week. My work will improve.'

Mr Reynolds: 'Good . . . yes, well done. Very good . . . Let the accounts department know the cost of this course and we'll pay for it.'

David: 'That's very kind of you, thank you. Apart from that are there any problems?'

Mr Reynolds: (smiles) 'No . . . no . . . you're doing well . . .'

David handles this brief interview well. Firstly he knows an appraisal interview is held after six months and he prepares for it. He obtained a copy of the appraisal form himself, asked himself the same type of questions Mrs Bradman would have considered and marked himself under each of the headings. He correctly identified his strengths (and, if appropriate, he would have mentioned them) and his weaknesses. He knew he was making mistakes on the new computer system. He identified the reason which was that he missed the training seminar. He then worked out how he could improve his work which was by reading a computer handbook and attending a short course.

When David goes to see Mr Reynolds he makes a special effort with his appearance. He is also punctual and polite. He doesn't sit down until he is invited to do so. David is friendly. He smiles, he looks at Mr Reynolds. He listens to him. He thinks Mr Reynolds is talking too much. David doesn't just want to sit there so he cuts in as soon as he can. 'Now it's my turn then!'

When David is shown the appraisal form he immediately sees that, as he expected, Mrs Bradman has indicated a weakness – 'David's recording and filing documentation of information is suspect'. Obviously, Mr Reynolds is going to quiz him on this so David is positive. He speaks first – 'May I explain?' He doesn't become shifty and evasive. He admits to a weakness. He states the reason – 'I was off sick on the day the training seminar was held'. He then explains how he will rectify the problem – 'I have just bought a handbook'. David concludes positively – 'My work *will* improve'.

After Mr Reynolds has indicated that Thompsons will pay for the course, David is again positive. He asks outright 'Are there any problems?' There are none.

You should prepare for an appraisal interview in the same way that David did. Try to obtain a copy of the appraisal form before the interview. If this is not possible, draft your own based on the job documents. Mark yourself realistically. What are your strengths? Develop these in the interview if you can (see David's selection interview with Mr Reynolds on page 75). Recognize your weaknesses, and face them. In an appraisal interview you will be asked about them. Consider why you are weak in those areas. Identify the reasons. Consider how you can improve, how you can turn these weaknesses into strengths.

In the interview, adhere to the Do's and Don'ts. Promote your strengths whenever possible. When asked about your weaknesses immediately apologise. It takes the heat out of the situation. Don't argue or contradict. Explain, as David did, why you are weak, tell the interviewer how you can improve and, as David did, prove that you intend to do this.

PROMOTION INTERVIEWS

Every ambitious employee wants to progress. At some stage, another job may become vacant or be created within the organization. When this happens you should approach job hunting and, hopefully, the interview in the same way you would approach any other job. Answer these questions.

- Is this job a step in the right direction?
- Can you do the job well?
- Do you have the experience required?
- Do you have the knowledge required?
- Do you have the skills required?
- Do you have the personality required?

If the answers to these questions are all yes then you should apply. Remember to:

- Research the organization.
- Research the job.
- Research the interview.
- Research any tests you might face.
- Research the interviewer.
- Think about the questions you may be asked.
- Adhere to the Do's and Don'ts.

TERMINATION INTERVIEWS

Instead of applying for another job within the same organization you may, of course, apply elsewhere. If you are successful you will need to hand in your notice.

If you intend to leave an organization, don't disappear without a word, ask a friend to pass on the news, or write a scribbled letter telling them that you're leaving. Tell your employer face to face. Explain why you are leaving. Make sure you leave on friendly terms.

Many employers conduct 'exit' interviews with employees who are leaving to find out their reasons. Such interviews often develop into arguments and bad feeling because the employee

77

wasn't direct and open in the first place. Don't wait to be asked to attend such an interview. Get there first!

David, for example, has now been at Thompsons for two years. As you know he wants to progress and become a sales agent. However, he realizes that, with Thompsons, he is unlikely to become one. All of their agents have been with them for many years and will, without doubt, be there for many more. David applies for a job with Thompsons' competitors, Harrisons, and is successful. He decides to be direct and open and immediately goes to see Mr Reynolds.

David: 'Hallo, Mr Reynolds, have you got a few minutes to spare?'

Mr Reynolds: 'Yes of course I have David. Sit down . . .'

David: (sits down and smiles)

Mr Reynolds: 'What can I do for you?'

David: 'I thought I should come in and tell you I've been offered a job as a sales representative with Harrisons which I'd like to accept.'

Mr Reynolds: 'I see . . . well this is a surprise I must say. I didn't know you were unhappy with us. You've never said anything have you?'

David: 'Well no I haven't but I'm not unhappy here Mr Reynolds. It's a good company, I like the people I work with. I like you. It's just that I want to become a sales agent and we both know my chances in that direction are limited here aren't they? Thompsons sales agents are all excellent.'

Mr Reynolds: 'You've not thought about moving into Advertising? Old Mr Sansom's due for retirement in a couple of years and between you and me I think you could do well in that department.'

David: 'Well that's very flattering Mr Reynolds and it's nice of you to say that but it's Sales I'm really interested in. Always has been. As I say, it's nothing personal at all. I'm happy here but I want to progress the way you have. You had to change companies to get where you are today didn't you?'

Mr Reynolds: 'Mmm, that's true . . . very true. I see what you mean . . . How much notice are you going to give us?'

David: 'Well I've told Harrisons I'll let them know later on today how soon I can start. I didn't want to say I could start next week if it would mean leaving you in the lurch. What do you think?'

Mr Reynolds: 'Two weeks would be better but we could cover for you if you wanted to leave in a week . . . I imagine John could stand in for you?'

David: 'Yes, definitely. He's very good – he wouldn't let you down.'

Mr Reynolds: 'Fine . . . fine. Well I'll be sorry to see you go David.'

David: 'Same here, Mr Reynolds. Thank you, incidentally, for all your help over the last couple of years.'

Mr Reynolds: 'My pleasure . . .'

David: 'It was appreciated.'

(They shake hands).

David catches Mr Reynolds at a good moment. He waits

until Mr Reynolds has finished his lunch and is in a good mood. David then comes straight to the point. He does not annoy or confuse Mr Reynolds by beating around the bush. Mr Reynolds, as you would expect, is surprised by the news. He questions David, and at this point the conversation could potentially develop into an argument. David, however, responds well. He takes the heat out of the situation by remaining friendly and calm. He praises the company, his colleagues and Mr Reynolds himself. He explains why he wants to leave and his reasons are logical and sensible. Mr Reynolds cannot take offence at David's comments. They are truthful.

Mr Reynolds then talks of Advertising but David again explains his plans. He again defuses the situation by stating that it is 'nothing personal'. To get Mr Reynolds on his side he then flatters him – 'I want to progress the way you have'. He wins him over by comparing his plans with Mr Reynolds' career – 'You had to change companies . . . didn't you?'

Of course, it is still important that David leaves on good terms and the final possible area of conflict is that of working out his notice. David indicates that he is flexible. He doesn't want to leave Mr Reynolds 'in the lurch'. At the same time he indicates that he would like to leave in a week. His approach is perfect.

Finally, David thanks Mr Reynolds for all his help over the last two years. He can now leave Thompsons knowing that he is highly thought of. Mr Reynolds, if approached by Harrisons, will give David a good reference. If David crosses paths with Thompsons again, he will be assured of a warm welcome.

RECOMMENDED READING

1. Anatasi, Anne   – *Psychological Testing* (Collier Mac-millan, 1988, £16.95).

2. Bell, Gordon   – *Secrets of Successful Speaking and Business Presentations* (Heinemann Professional, 1988, £14.95).

3. Maitland, Iain   – *How to Win at Job Hunting* (Business Books, 1989, £4.95).

4. Mandel, Steve   – *Effective Presentation Skills* (Kogan Page, 1988, £3.95)

5. Marks, W.   – *How to Give a Speech* (Institute of Personnel Management, 1979, £3.25).

6. Miller, Kenneth M   – *Psychological Testing in Personnel Assessment* (Gower Press, 1975, £22.50).

7. Turk, Christopher   – *Effective Speaking* (Spon, 1985, £8.50).

INDEX

Index